Foreword

Thank you very much for choosing this book!

Hi! Would you like to deepen your knowledge and skills of CAD design with Fusion 360 from Autodesk? Then you've come to the right place! Because based on 10 simple to moderately difficult design projects, you will learn new approaches and new features in Fusion 360 in this hands-on course and thus improve your CAD skills. Take this course if you already have entry-level knowledge of Fusion 360 and have already taken the entry-level course on it. If not, please take a look at the Beginner course *"Fusion 360 | Step-by-Step"* first. I am an engineer and would like to teach you the fantastic program Fusion 360 in a simple and easy to understand way. By the way, you can use Fusion 360 as a private user with a hobby license for FREE!

Here is the link to download:

https://www.autodesk.de/products/fusion-360/free-trial

This detailed and hands-on course is specifically designed for intermediate to advanced users and shows in detail and step by step how to succeed in more complex CAD designs. In this course, you will find 10 great 3D objects that you can design along and step by step. Get your copy of the course now and start improving your Fusion 360 skills today!

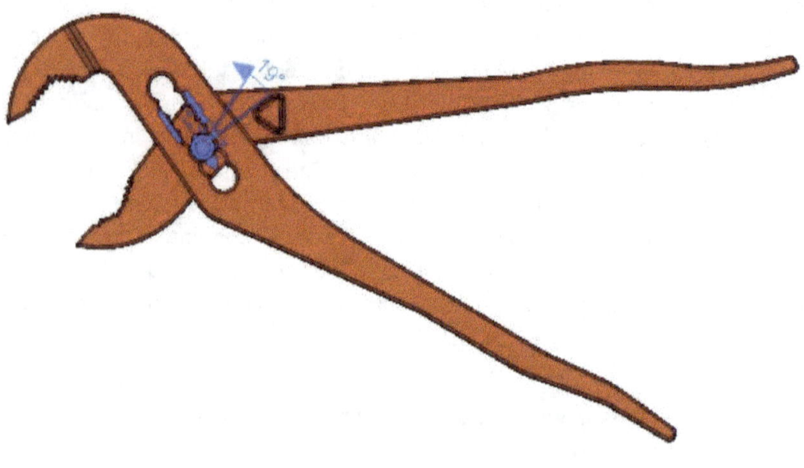

Table of contents

Legal information 1

Foreword 2

Table of contents 3

1 Introduction: course scope and software.................................4

1.1 What to expect and what you will learn in this course 4

1.2 Fusion 360 and program download....................................5

Section I: Simple design projects **7**

2 Project 1: Helical spring...7

3 Project 2: Hexagon socket bolt......................................10

4 Project 3: Gear...18

5 Project 4: Flower vase 31

6 Project 5: Slotted screwdriver.......................................37

7 Project 6: Wrench (open-end wrench)...............................45

Section II: Medium difficulty design projects................... **53**

8 Project 7: Ball bearing 53

9 Project 8: Watering can 72

10 Project 9: Remote control 86

11 Project 10: Water pump pliers 103

Closing words.. **122**

1 Introduction: course scope and software

1.1 What to expect and what you will learn in this course

Hello and welcome to the Fusion 360 Advanced Course | Part 1!
Thank you for choosing this course!

In this course, you'll find 10 great design projects of easy to moderate difficulty that you can create step-by-step in Autodesk's Fusion 360 for expanding your CAD skills. This course is as hands-on as it gets. As an advanced user, you don't need a big introduction to the program, you'll certainly want to get started right away. That's why, after a short note on how to download the program, we'll start immediately with the first design project.

As you know, Autodesk's Fusion 360 not only lets you design, but also simulate, render, animate and more in one platform. However, this course is specifically for advanced CAD only. You will find separate courses for each of the other areas as you progress. So, the main focus of this course is on advanced CAD design with Fusion 360!

In this course, aimed specifically at intermediate to advanced users, you will learn how to make the most of Fusion 360 to design great 3D objects. So in this course we will deal with easy projects, such as a hexagon socket bolt, a screwdriver, a flower vase and moderately difficult projects, such as a ball bearing, a remote control and a pipe wrench. But that was just a small sample, there are more great projects just waiting for you. Each 3D object will be created step-by-step and one-by-one in this course, giving you an easy introduction to the design approaches and thus making you more familiar with more Fusion 360 features with each project.

If you have <u>no</u> beginner knowledge or have <u>never</u> worked with Fusion 360 before, you should definitely work through the beginner course: *"Fusion 360 | Step-by-Step"*. This will give you a simple and easy to understand introduction to the program. If you have already completed this course, you are well-prepared for the upcoming design projects!

Briefly, this course will teach you in detail:

- To reinforce the basic features of Fusion 360 in use as well as beginner knowledge.
- Learn new 2D and 3D features
- Design in a practice-oriented manner using example projects
- New approaches in design
- Create individual parts and assemblies

- **Implement simple design projects:**
- *Coil spring,*
- *Hexagon socket bolt,*
- *Gear,*
- *Flower vase,*
- *Slotted screwdriver,*
- *Wrench.*
- **Implement moderately difficult design projects:**
- *Ball bearing,*
- *Watering can,*
- *Remote control,*
- *Pipe wrench.*

It is best to stay in the order given by the course, as the lessons in this course also build on each other somewhat. Be sure to complete the corresponding beginner's course first, since basics are not mentioned in this course for the time being. However, here and there we will encounter them again in the course and in this way intuitively contribute to the deepening of the already existing design knowledge. After a short chapter on downloading the program and on alternative programs, we will immediately get started with the first project!

1.2 Fusion 360 and program download

Fusion 360 from Autodesk offers a clear and simple user interface and is also available free of charge for private users as a so-called personal license! This version has a somewhat limited range of functions, but is perfectly adequate for private and hobby users. For all users who want to use Fusion 360 commercially, there is a paid full version, starting at currently $60 per month. After creating an account with Autodesk, you can choose either version after comparing the feature set. But as mentioned before, if you are a private or hobby user, you can definitely pick the free version! Here you have to cut back in the area of "Generative Design" and "Simulation" because for the use of these two functions you need a paid license, but for hobby and private users these are often not necessary at all. However, as a home user, you can also simply start with the free version and still upgrade later if necessary. You can download Fusion 360 directly online after creating a user account.

The structure of the design features is relatively identical in all common CAD programs that are used as an engineer or technician in everyday work. Mostly, other **professional** CAD program licenses like "SolidWorks", "CATIA", "Solid Edge" or "AutoCAD" and "Autodesk Inventor" are used, which cost one to several thousand Euros and are therefore usually only worthwhile for professional users and self-employed persons. Here, however, you can at least typically obtain a trial version for 30 days or even more. As a student, you also have the option of obtaining a free student license for most CAD programs for the duration of your studies.

And now we're off to the races! In the first section, we will deepen our CAD knowledge and the handling of Fusion 360 through easy design projects. To achieve this, we'll start with a very simple project, creating a coil spring. But don't worry, the difficulty level increases with each project, so there should be something for everyone! Let's go!

Section I: Simple design projects

2 Project 1: Helical spring

Now we are already starting with the first design project! To warm up, we create a helical spring, which already looks a bit more complicated at first glance.

However, since there is an extra function for this in Fusion 360, this will be a breeze. The function is called "Coil" and is located in the "Create" menu.

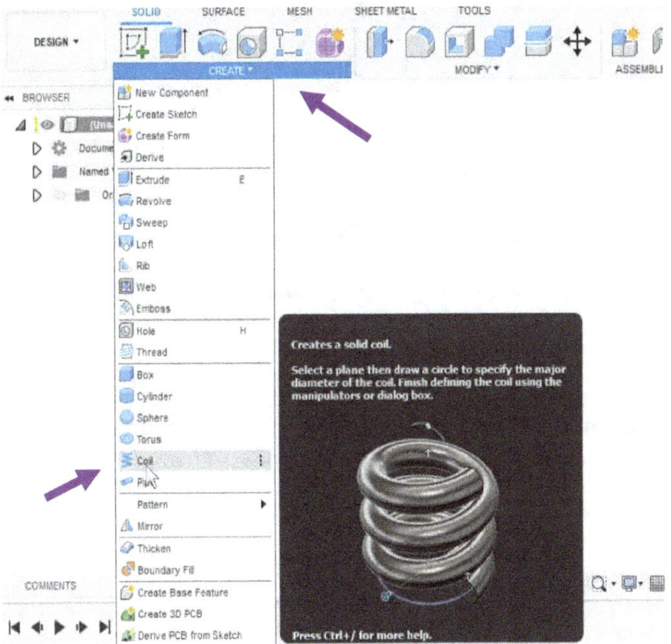

To create a helical spring, we must then first select a plane and sketch the diameter. For example, we select the x-y plane and set the diameter to 10 mm.

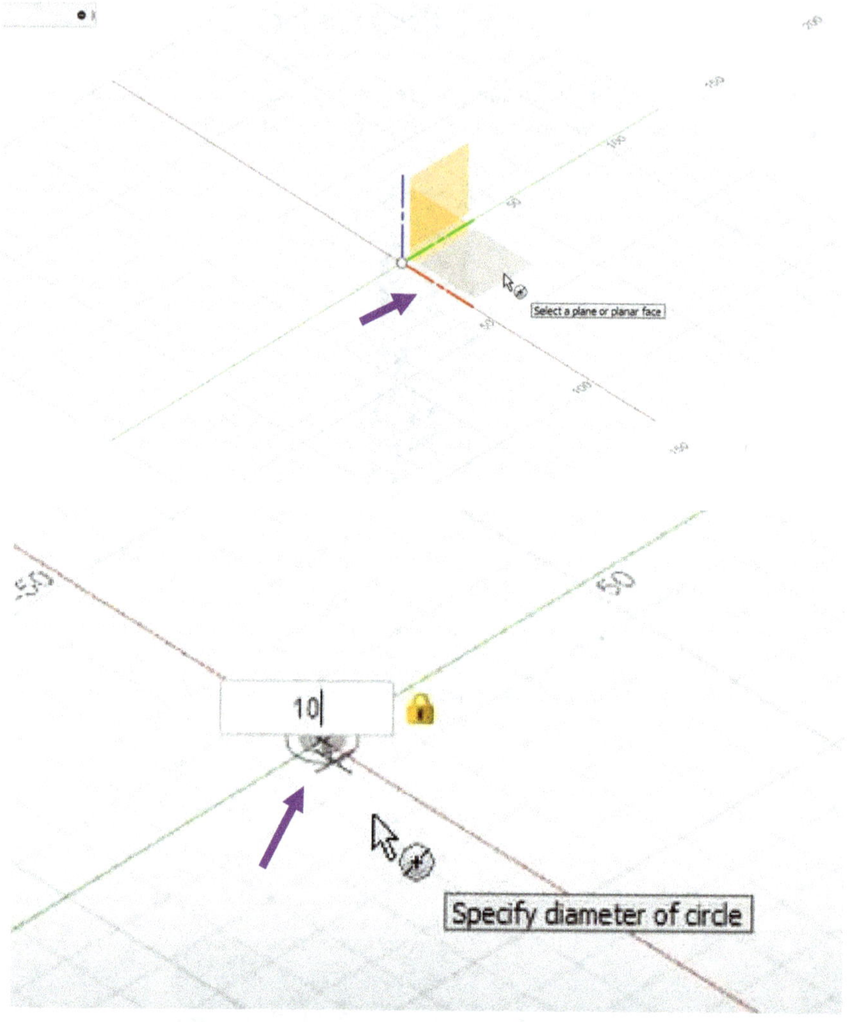

Then the program already creates a helical spring for us. We can then make settings for height, turns and more. For example, we could choose 40 mm as the height.

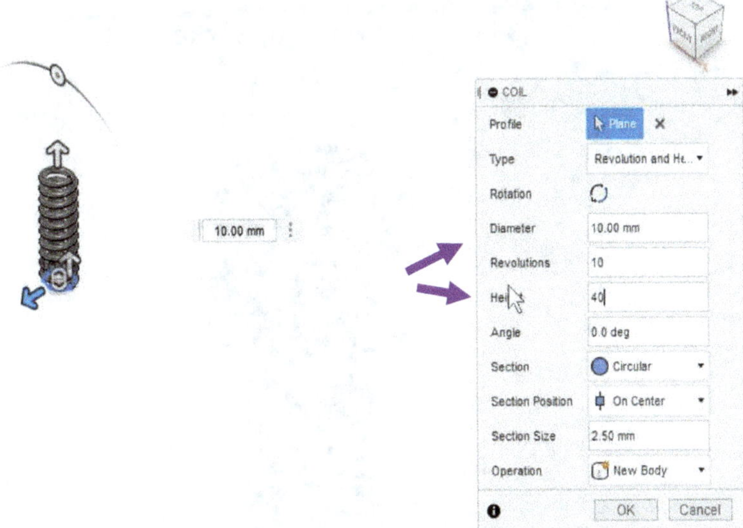

And then the spring is also already finished. As I said, this project was really very simple and just meant to warm up. Don't worry, the level of difficulty increases with each project. There are still many great and sometimes complex projects waiting for you! As a following project, we will create a hexagon socket bolt with all details.

3 Project 2: Hexagon socket bolt

In this second design project, we want to increase the level of difficulty slightly and design an M8 x 30 hexagon socket bolt with full thread length. We can find the dimensions for this on the Internet or in a mechanical engineering table book or standard parts catalog. We can design this screw in two ways. Firstly, with the help of one or more extrusions, and secondly, with the help of the "Revolve" function as a turned part. We will use the latter way because it leads to the goal faster. To do this, we first need one half of the cross-section of the screw. You can imagine that you cut the screw in the middle. We need to draw one half of the profile, which can then be seen. To achieve this, we create a sketch on the x-z plane and draw a 4 mm long horizontal line and a 30 mm long vertical line following it.

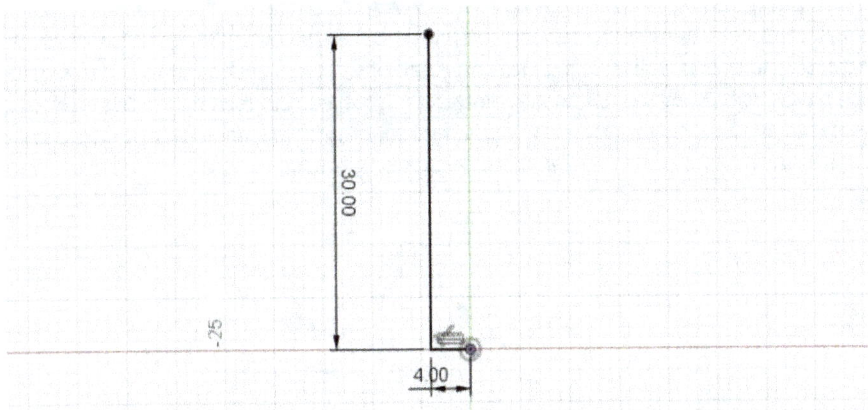

This is the shaft of the screw. For the head we need a 2.5 mm horizontal line, an 8 mm vertical line and another 6.5 mm horizontal line. Finally, we connect the top point with the bottom point using a vertical line so that the profile is completely closed.

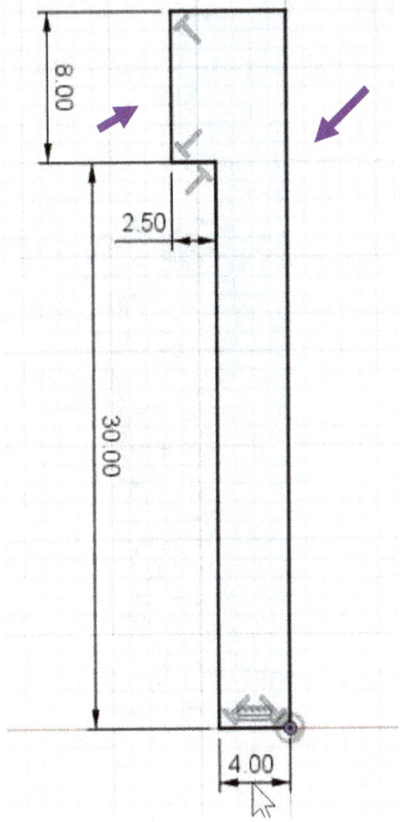

As you can see from the black color, the profile is also fully defined. Please always pay attention to this as well. This profile is now half of the cross-section of the screw. After we have finished the sketch, we can rotate the profile around an axis in 3D mode. To do this, we select the profile and the function "Revolve". Then we have to select an axis around which we want to rotate. In our case, this is the blue z-axis.

The base body of the screw is now created.

Before creating the thread, we first add fillets and chamfers as follows: we round the edges of the head with 0.5 mm each using the "Fillet" function.

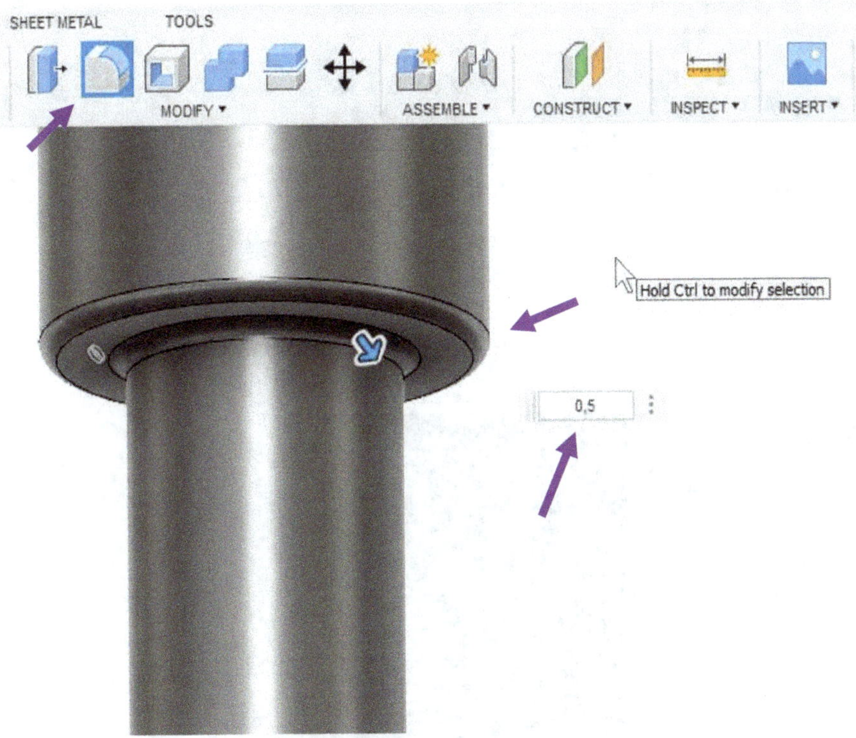

For the lowest edge, we create a 1 mm chamfer with "Chamfer".

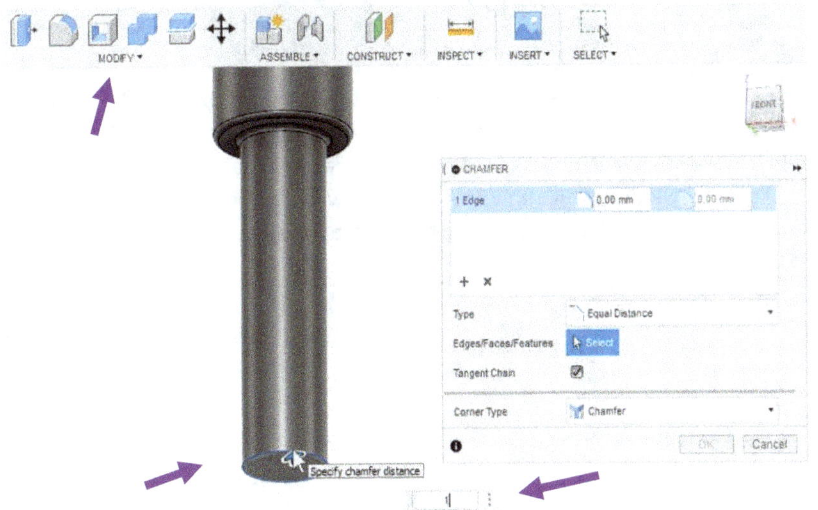

In the next step, we dedicate ourselves to the thread, which we can create with the function "Thread" in the menu "Create".

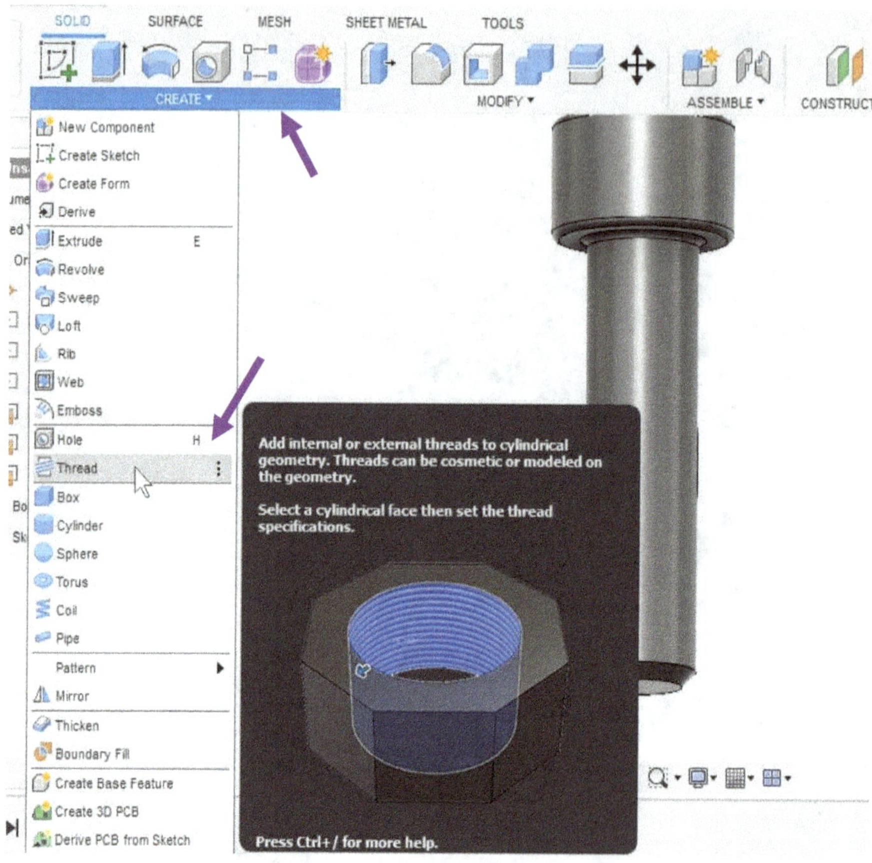

Simply select the function, select a surface, in this case the shaft, and set the thread parameters in the settings. We want a thread over the whole length, so activate "Full Length", as well as a real model of the thread instead of a mere graphic representation, so we activate "Modeled". It should be a M8 screw, the appropriate size is already set: M8 x 1.25. Make sure that an isometric thread profile is set. Excellent!

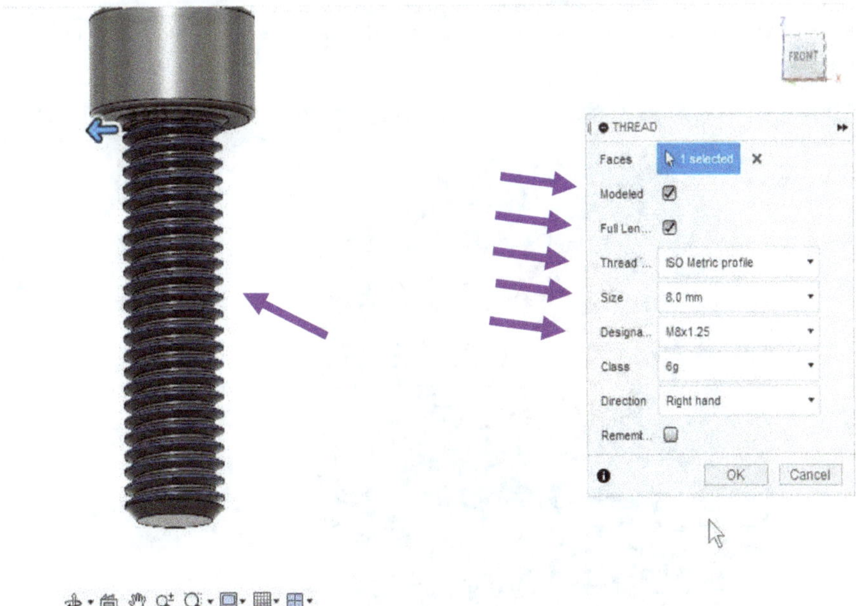

Almost finished! Now we still need the hexagon socket profile to hold the tool. To do this, we first create a hole on the top surface of the screw head with the "Hole" function. It should be a simple hole, without thread. The hole should be 4 mm deep and have a diameter of 6 mm.

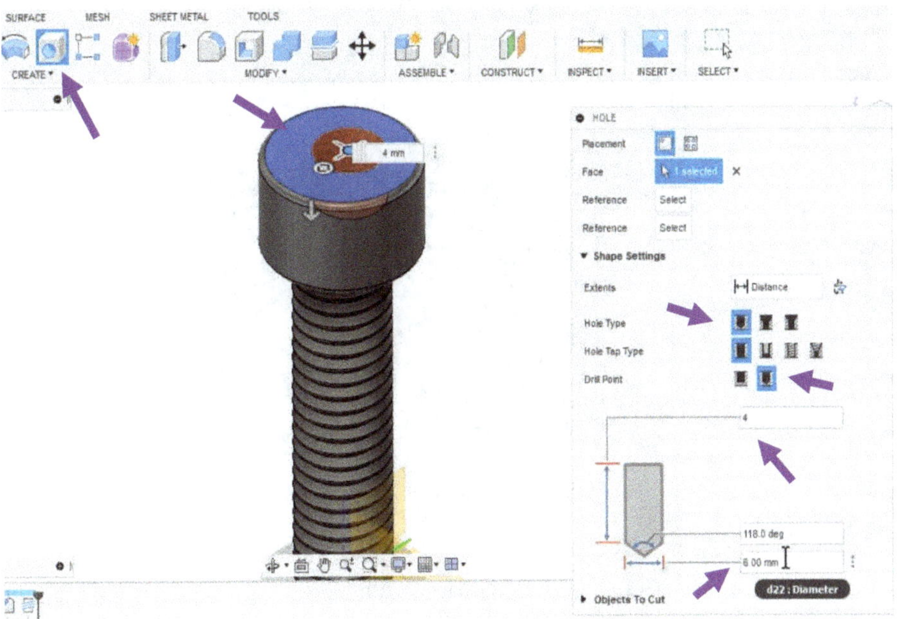

Finally, we determine the position by dragging the center of the hole to the center of the screw head.

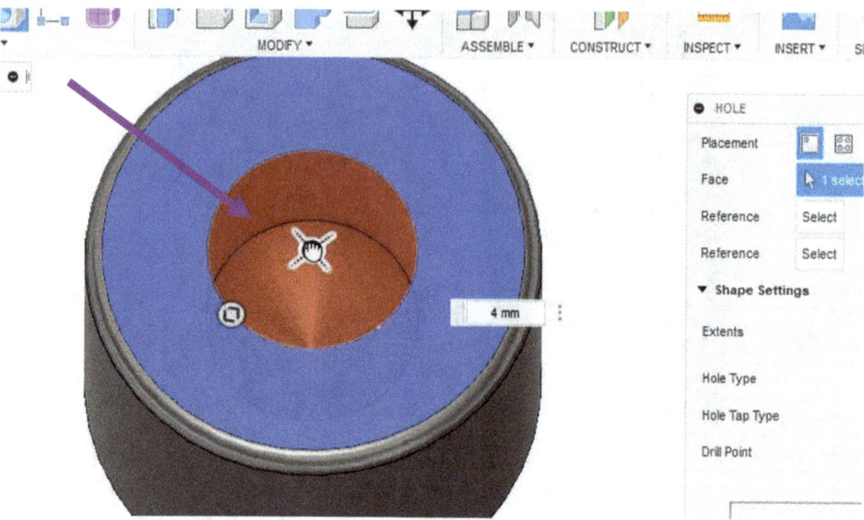

In the next step, we create the hexagon socket profile. To do this, we draw a polygon on the top surface of the screw head, which can be found in the "Create" menu. We need an "inscribed polygon".

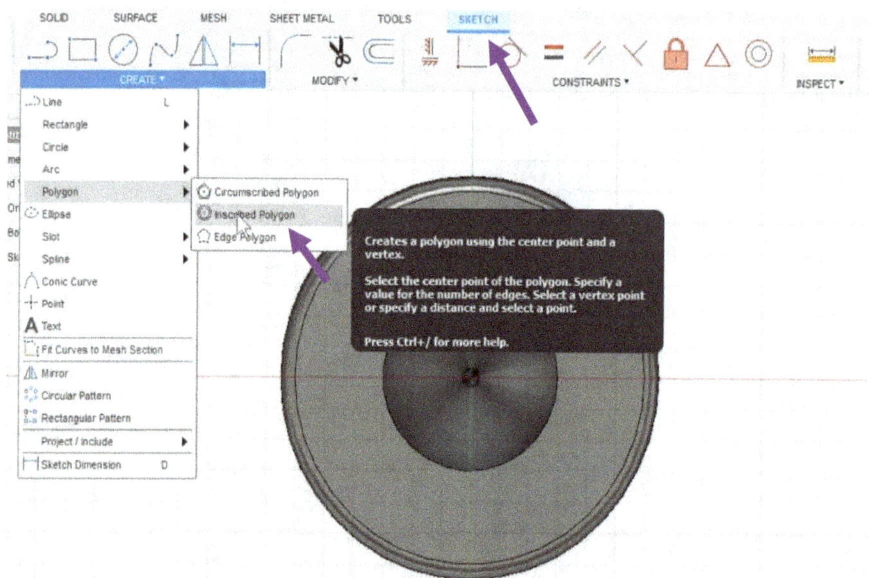

Simply draw the circle and attach a dimension. We need 6 mm between the edges of the polygon.

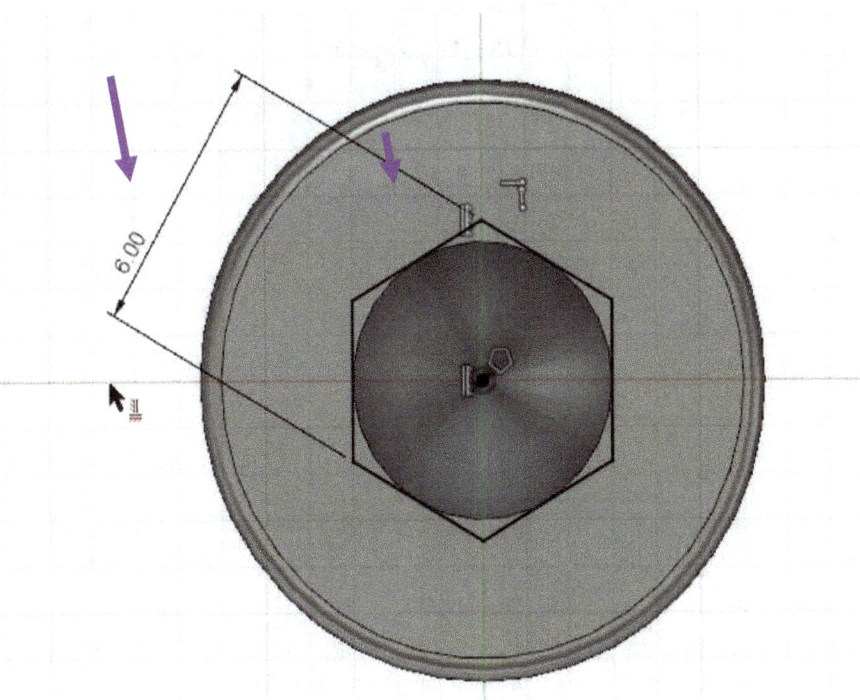

To define the profile completely, we still set the upper corner point in vertical relation to the origin. Now we can close the sketch. Then we select the "Extrusion" function and the remaining sections of the hexagonal profile and extrude them with -4 mm.

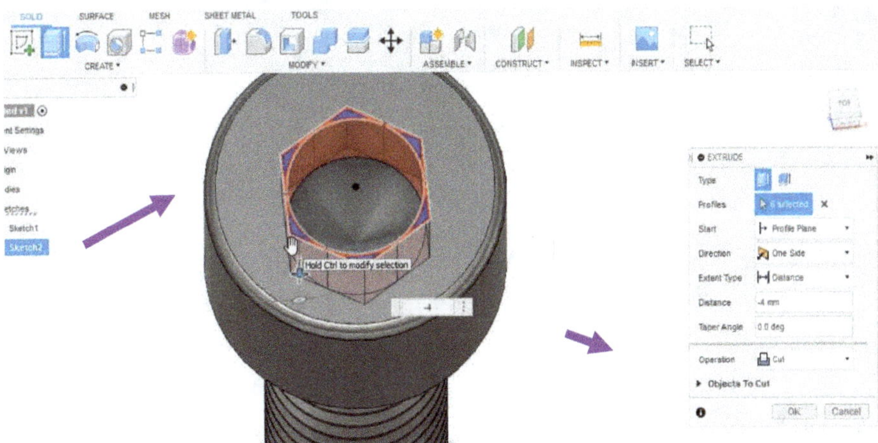

The program then automatically switches to the "Cut" setting and cuts away material. The hexagon socket bolt is finished.

4 Project 3: Gear

As our next project, we would like to design a gear, which could be part of a more complex machine, for example. For the gear wheel we proceed as follows: We create the basic body for the gear, already including the teeth and the receptacle in the center, completely in only one sketch to work as efficiently as possible. To achieve this, we sketch on the x-y plane to look at the component from above. For the base body, we first need a 50 mm circle.

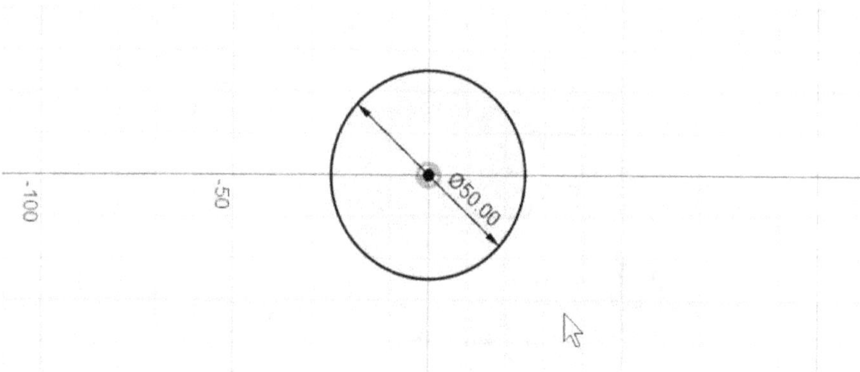

We will then cut out the teeth of the gear from this basic body. To do this, we sketch the first tooth in the upper area. We first draw only one half of the tooth and then mirror it. For this, we need a 1 mm horizontal line.

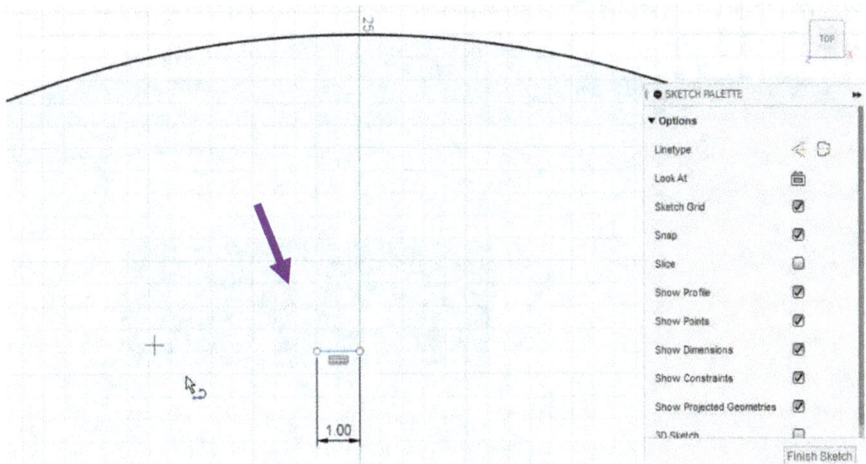

Then follows a second, oblique line.

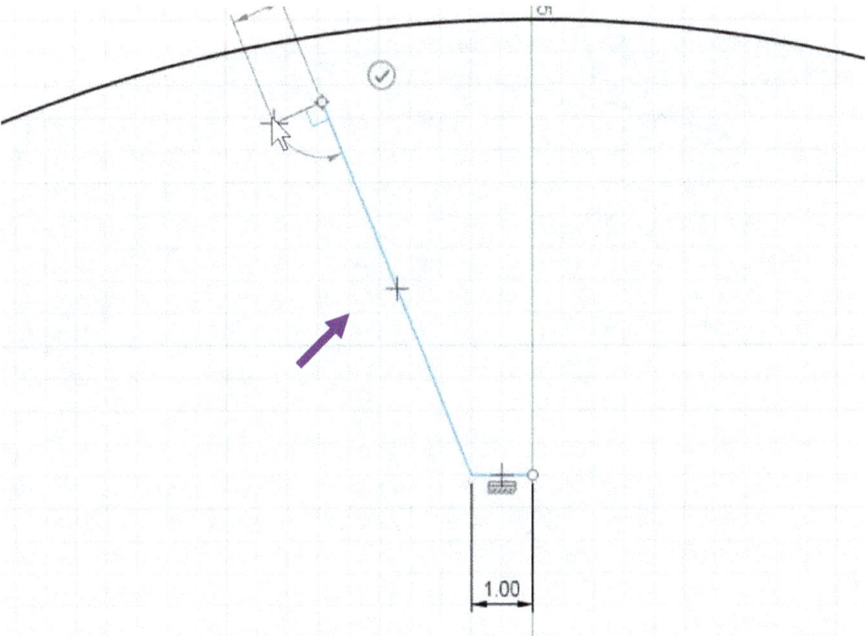

In the upper area we then add a tangent arc, whose start and end points should sit on the circle on the one hand, and on the end point of the oblique line on the other.

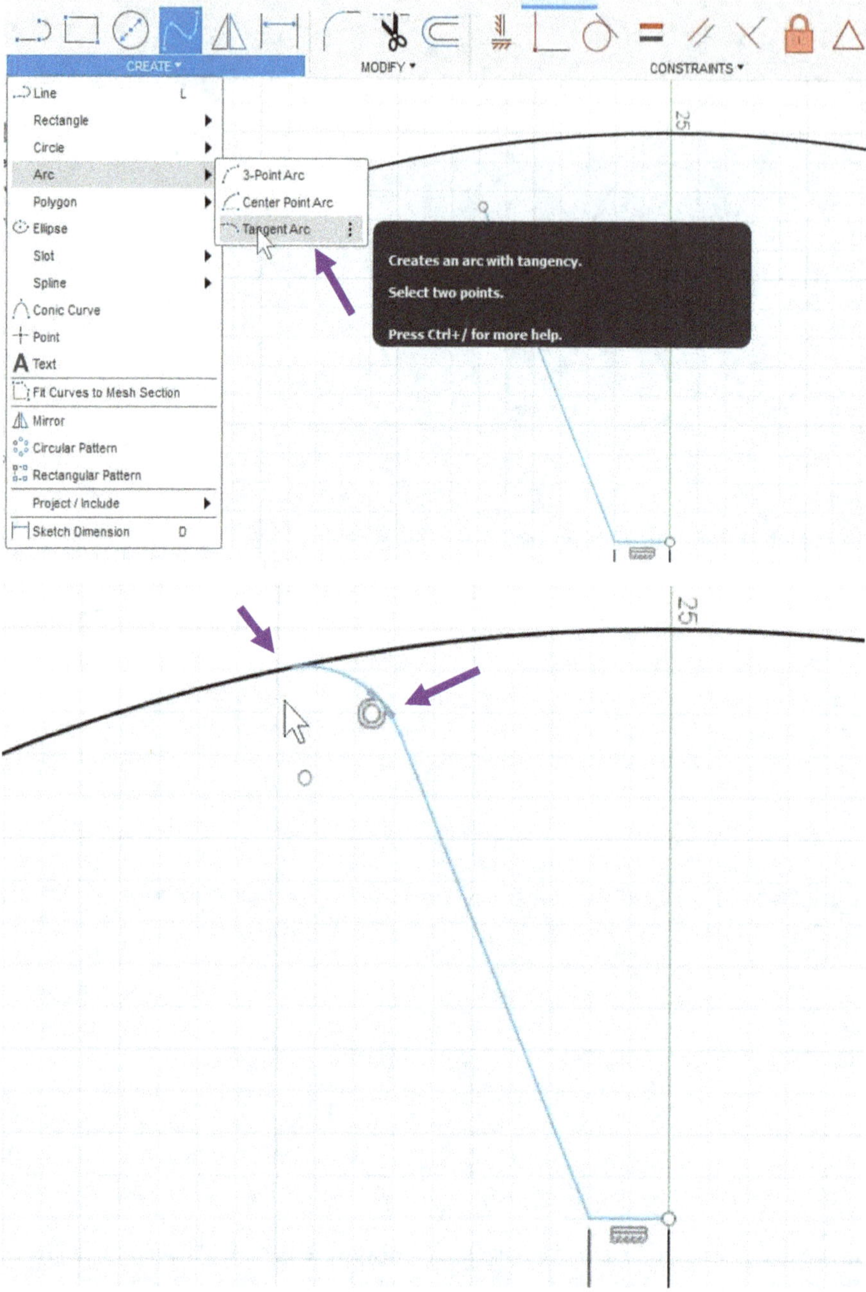

We then dimensioned the distance in the vertical direction between the corner point of the tangent arc and the starting point of the first line as 3 mm.

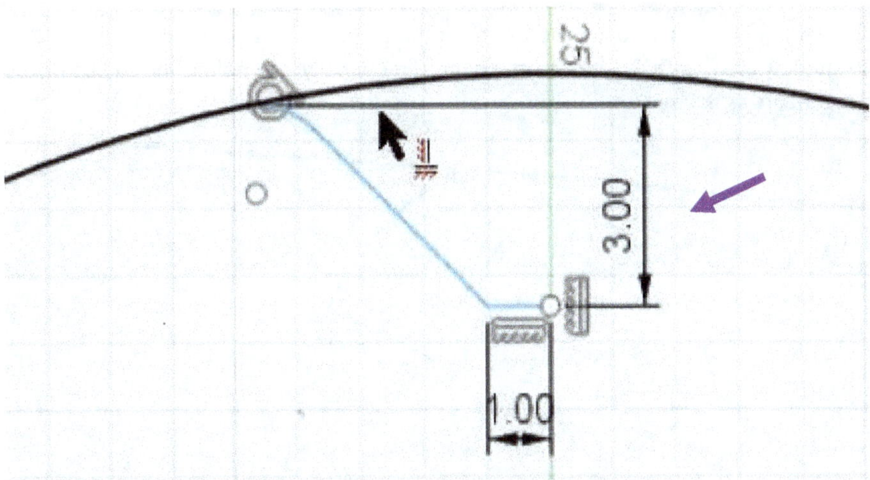

Then we vertically link the starting point of the first drawn line with the origin, and horizontally dimension a distance of 2 mm between the corner point of the tangent arc and the starting point of the first line.

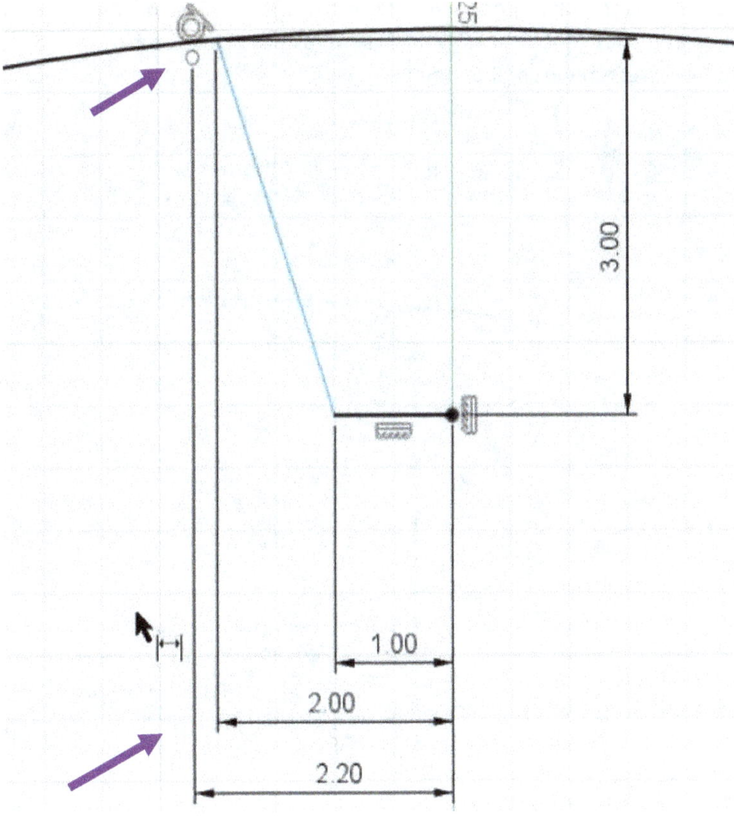

In addition, we dimensioned the center of the tangent arc, which is currently located in the left area, with 2.2 mm to the centerline. Finally, we define the radius of the tangent arc as 0.5 mm.

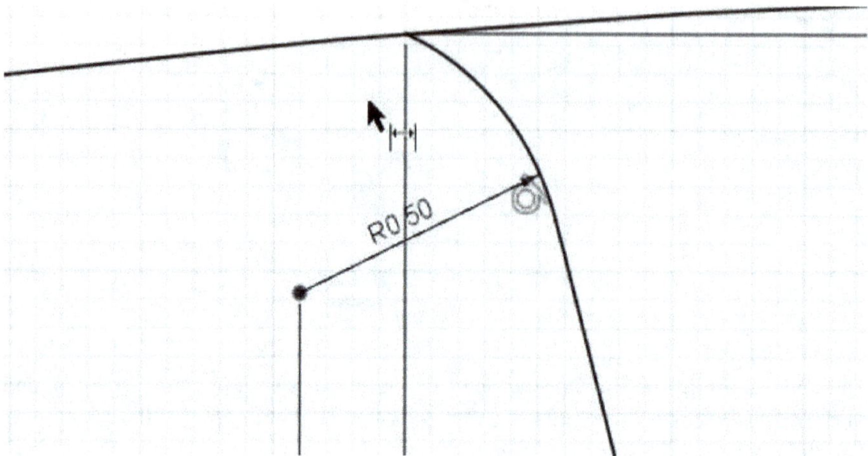

Now the profile is completely defined and can be mirrored. First, however, we integrate a rounding in the lower-left area. To do this, we use the "Fillet" function already in the 2D area and enter a radius of 0.5 mm.

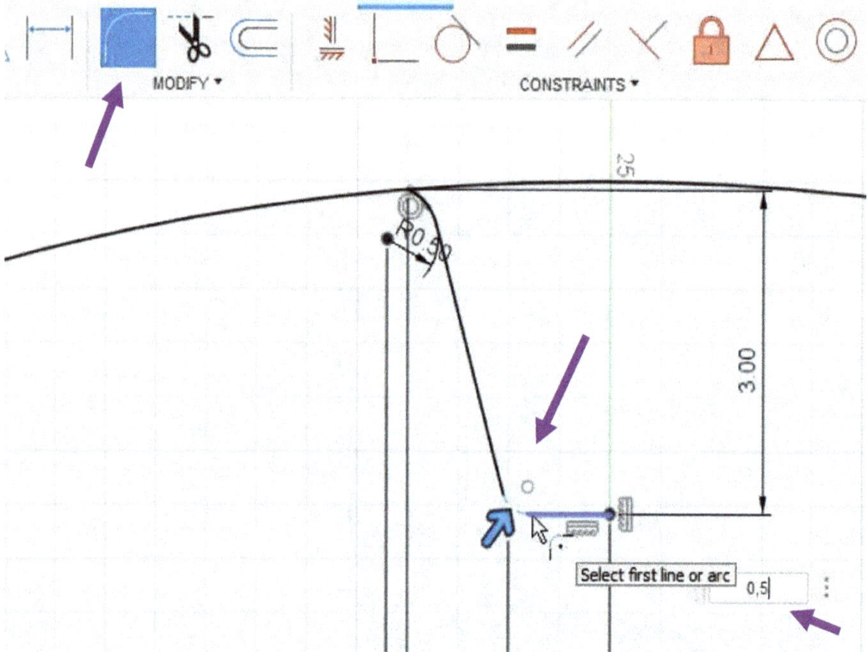

To understand, we could have drawn the tooth of the gear without fillets and then filleted it in 3D mode. However, since we need a lot of these teeth, we will save ourselves a lot of work by creating the tangent arc and fillet at this early step. Now, to mirror the profile, we still need a mirror axis, which we create from a line that we right-click to turn into a design geometry.

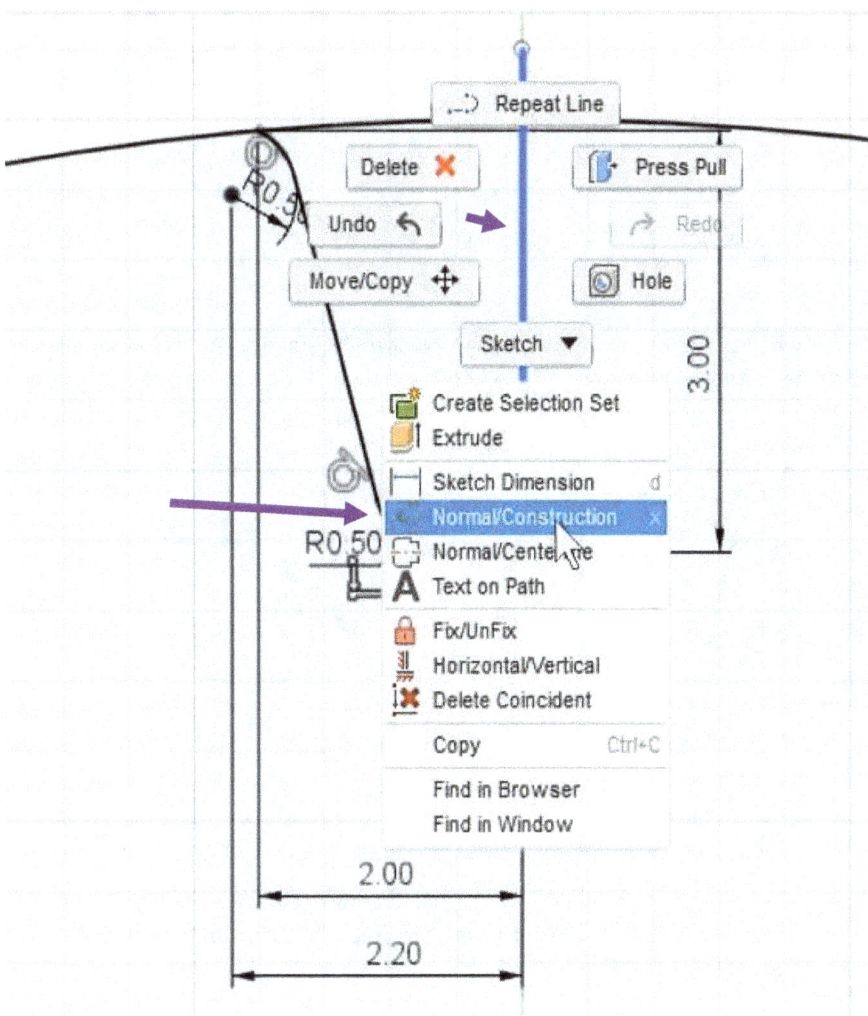

Then we select the "Mirror" function from the "Create" section and first select the objects to be mirrored.

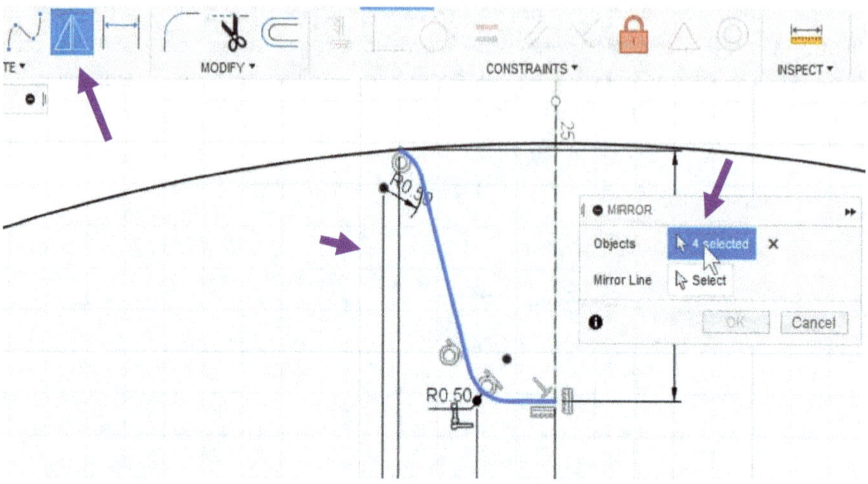

Then switch the selection in the settings to Mirror axis and select the vertical design line. The first tooth is ready.

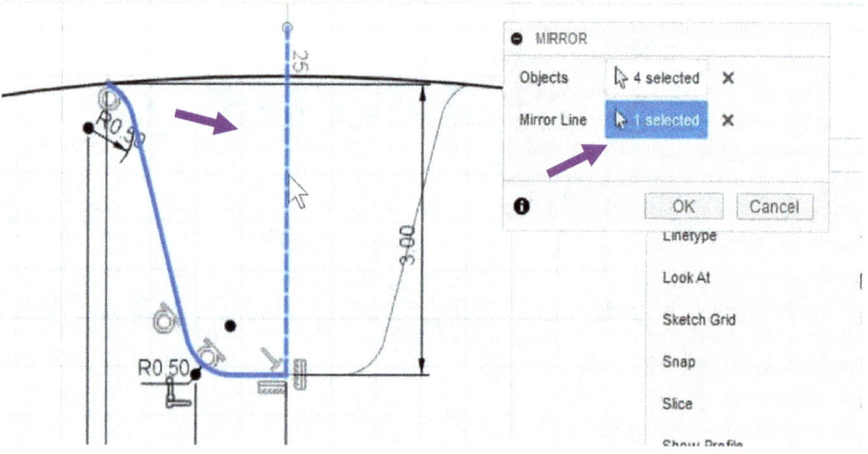

Now, in order not to have to draw more than 20 more teeth, we use the "Pattern" or "Circular Pattern" function, which allows us to create a circular pattern or copies in a circular arrangement.

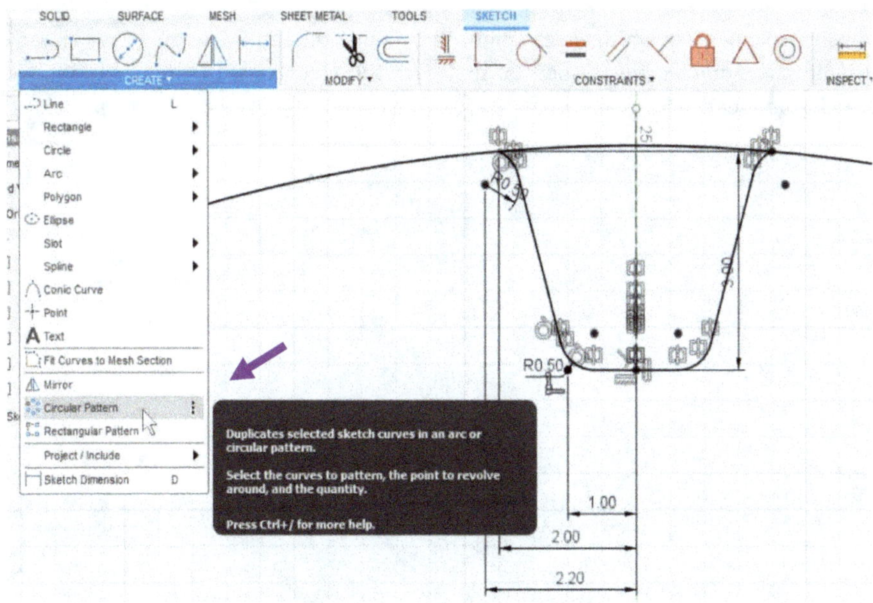

To do this, first select all the lines and arcs of the first tooth, change the selection in the settings to "Center Point" and then select the center of the circle (origin).

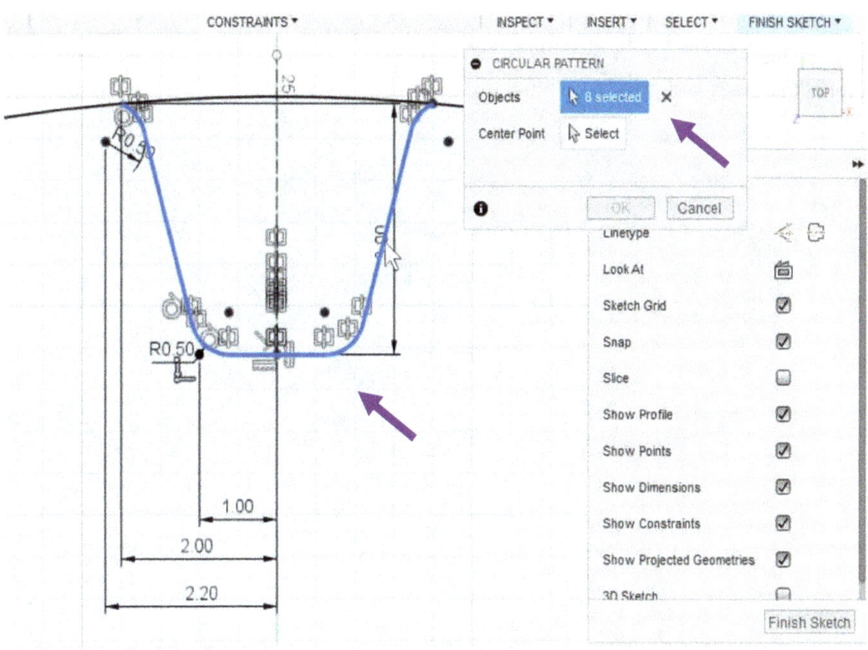

A window appears in which we can enter the number of teeth we want. I have already tried out the number in advance. So that each tooth connects to another tooth, we need a number of 25.

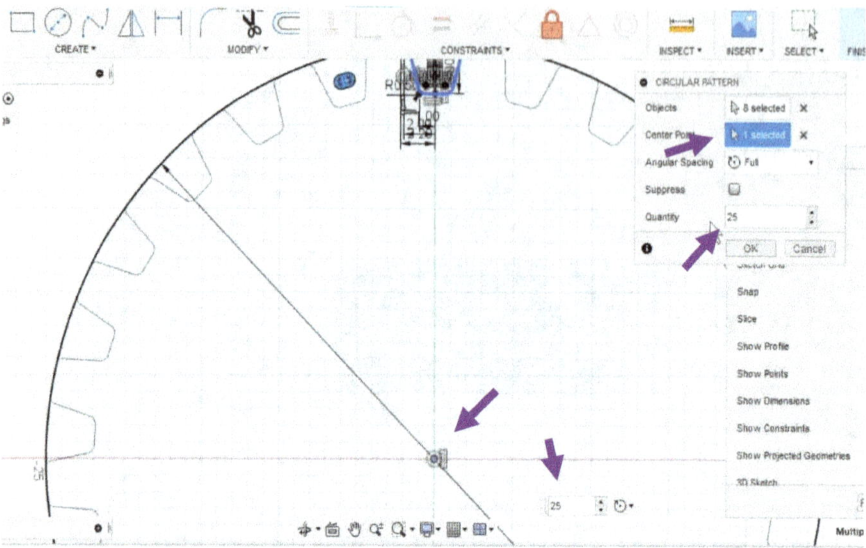

Confirm with "Ok". As you can see, this pattern function has simplified the design for us considerably. Now we only have to remove the upper boundaries between the individual teeth with the "Trim" function, and then we get the first part of the gear.

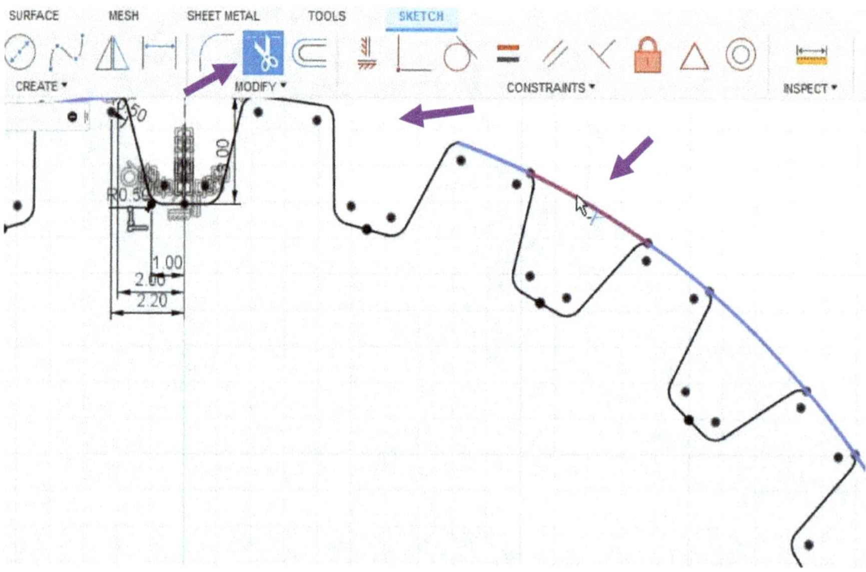

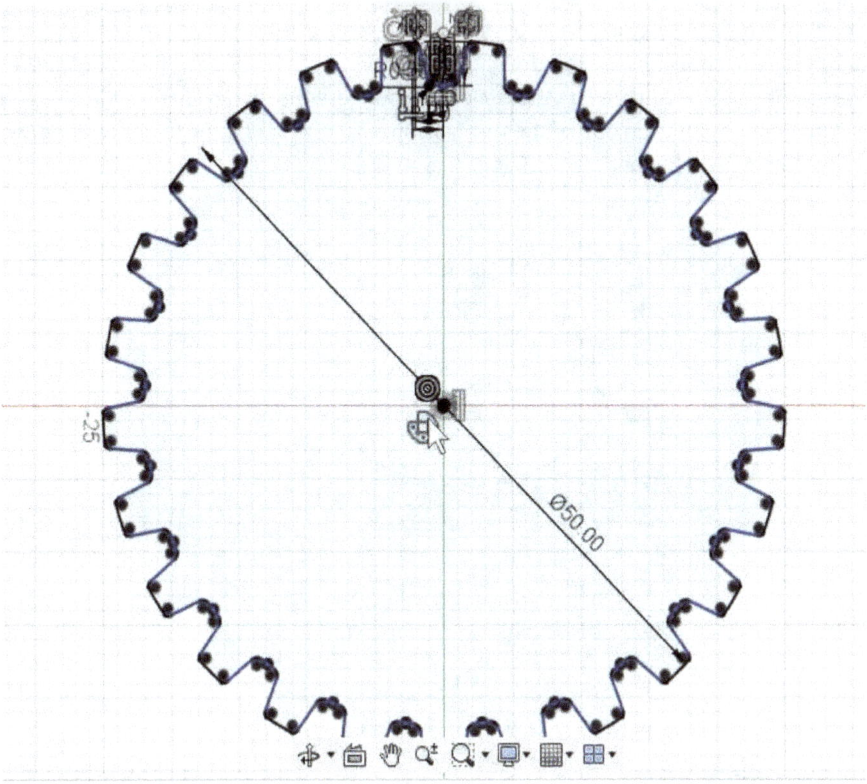

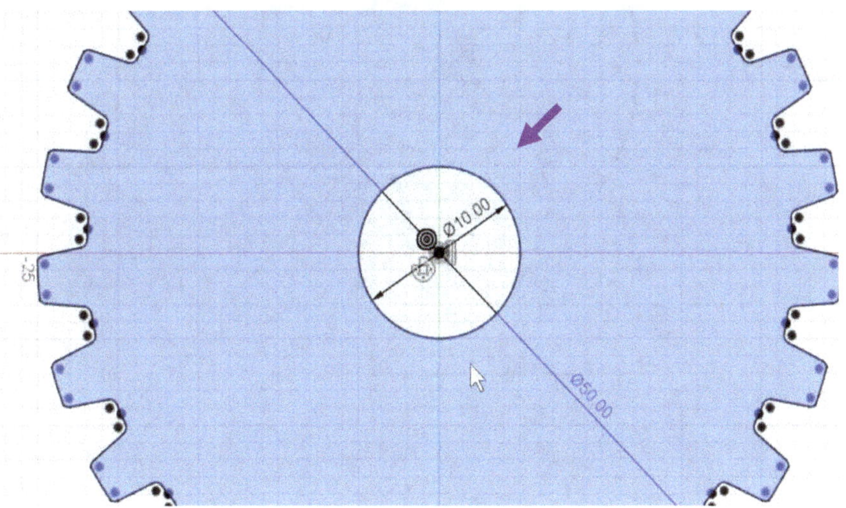

For the second part of the gear, the hole, or cutout for a shaft with drive nose, we first need a circle with 10 mm diameter in the center.

We then create the rectangular cutout for a drive nose using a 3 mm vertical line whose starting point should be on the circle, followed by a 4 mm horizontal line and another vertical line that should end on the circle and complete the rectangular profile. We add a 2 mm dimension from one of the two side lines to the origin, and finally remove the superfluous circle segment with "Trim".

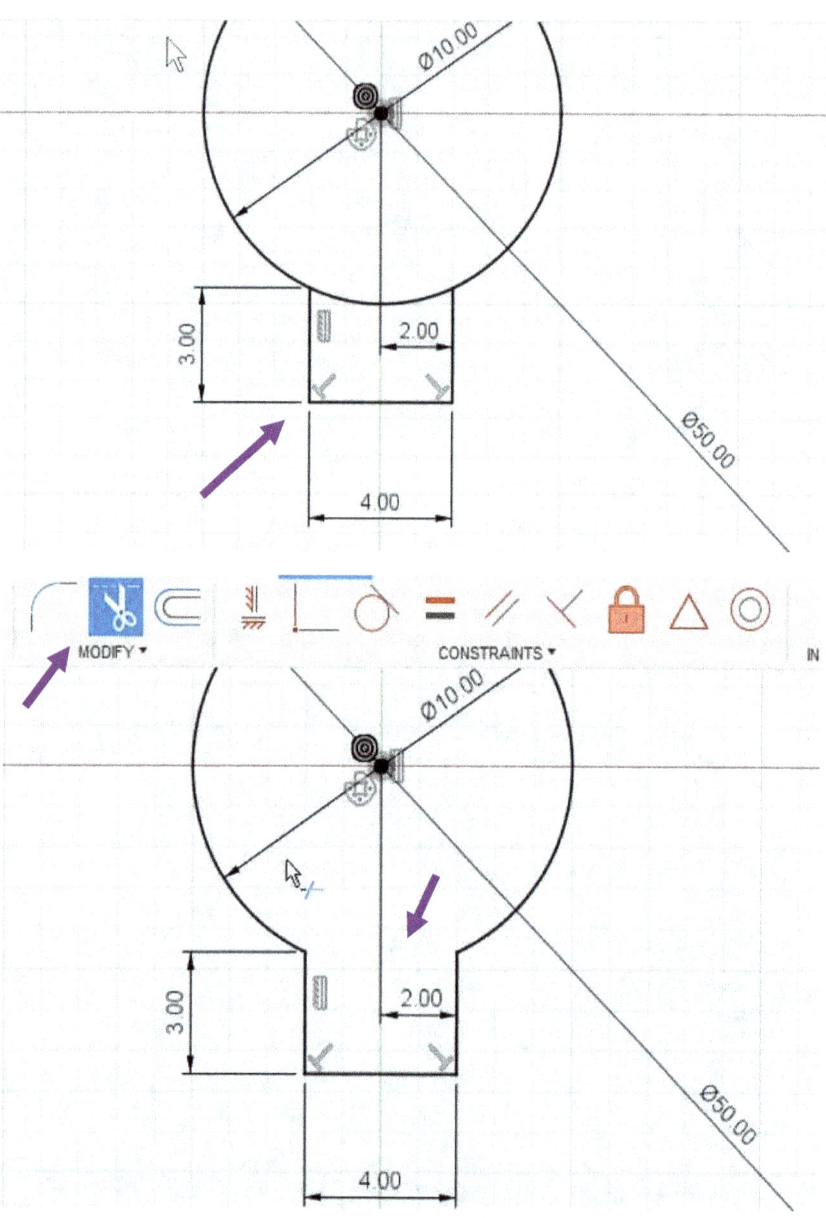

Now the complete basic body of the gear is ready in the 2D area and can be extruded in the 3D area with "Extrude" 10 mm.

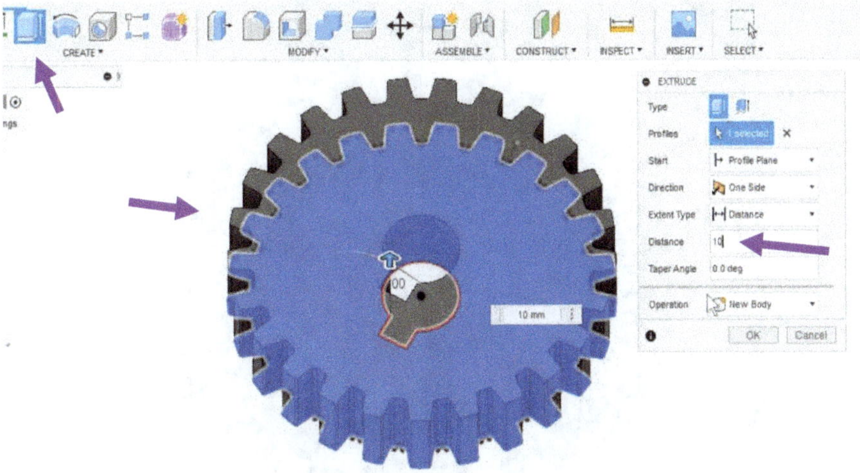

Now we also see that we no longer need to create fillets at the edges of the individual teeth of the gear in an elaborate and manual manner, since these are already present due to our profile geometry.

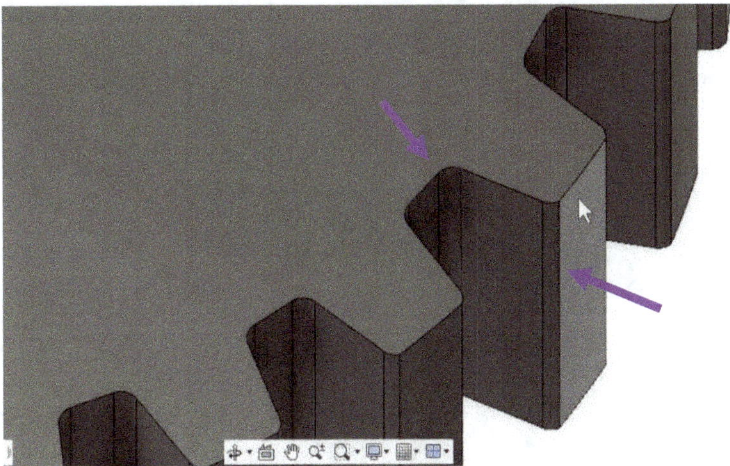

We only need a fillet for the surrounding edges of the two cover surfaces, which we can create quickly and easily with "Fillet". Simply select both surfaces and enter 0.2 mm, for example.

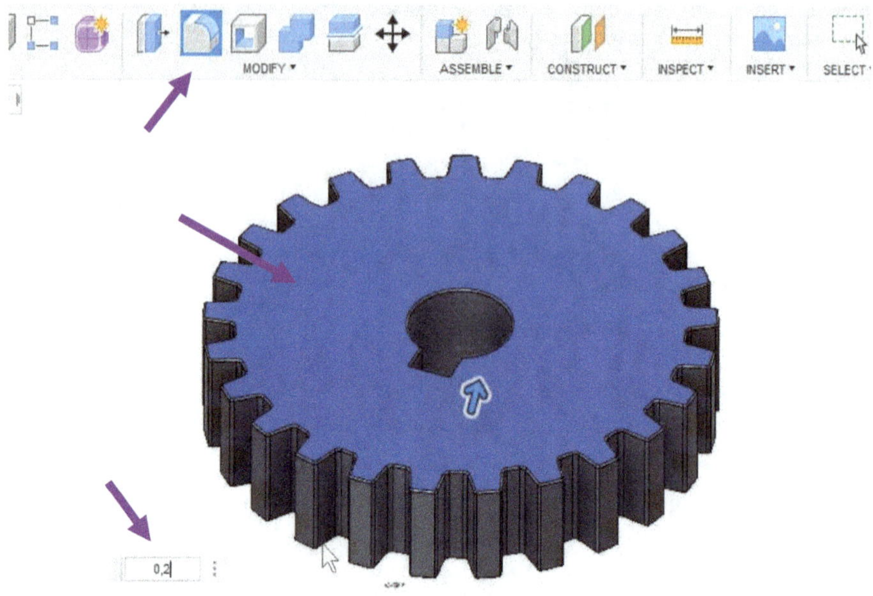

We made it! After a short breather, we're off to the next project! We will create an artistic flower vase. By the way, in the second section, i.e., in the moderately difficult design projects, there will also be a few more general objects, such as a remote control or a watering can, and not just technical design projects, as is the case for the most part in this section.

5 Project 4: Flower vase

Welcome back! In this project, we will design a fancy flower vase, which we will build as a simple rotational part. To do this, we'll start a sketch, say on the x-z plane, and again draw half of the cross-section of the vase, as we did with the screw. For this, we start with a 250 mm long vertical line, which is the center line of our design. We dimension the upper end point at a distance of 85 mm from the origin and link the line "coincident" to the origin so that it is completely defined.

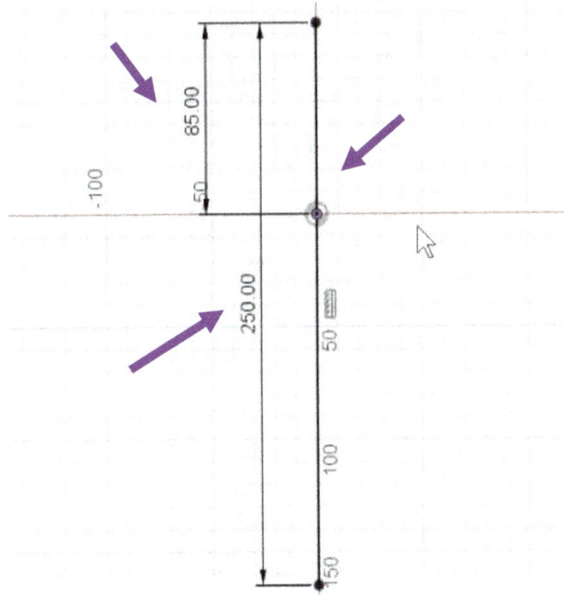

We then sketch the top and bottom horizontal boundary lines of our vase, with 35 mm for the top line and 45 mm for the bottom line.

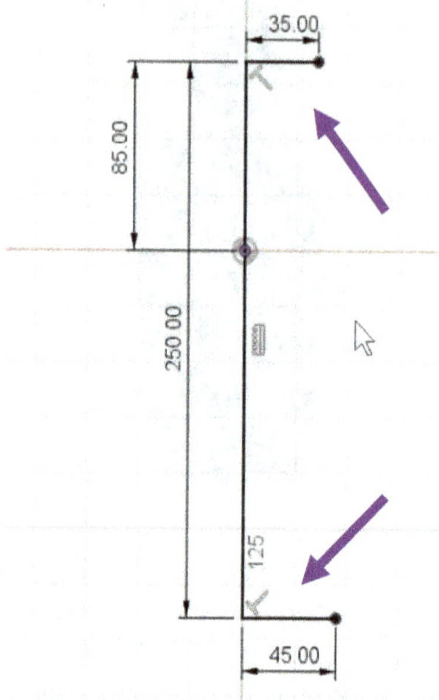

Then follow more horizontal lines that will serve as auxiliary lines, that is, design lines for the outer wall of the vase. One line with 25 mm and one line with 55 mm.

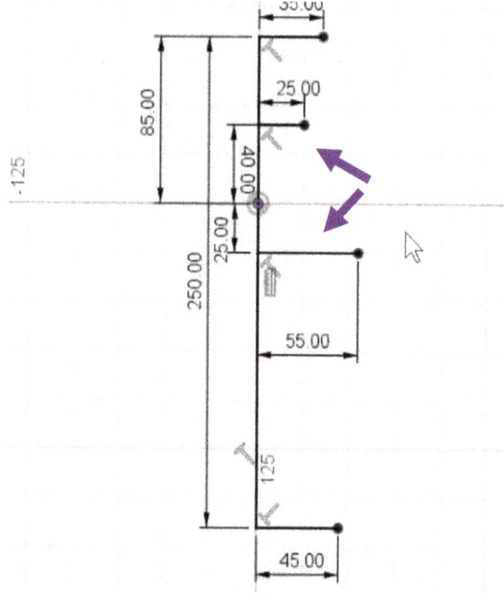

The 25 mm line gets a distance of 40 mm to the origin and the other line gets a distance of 25 mm to the origin. We still set the two line starting points coincident to the vertical one, if this relation was not set during drawing. After conversion to design lines, we draw connecting lines as shown.

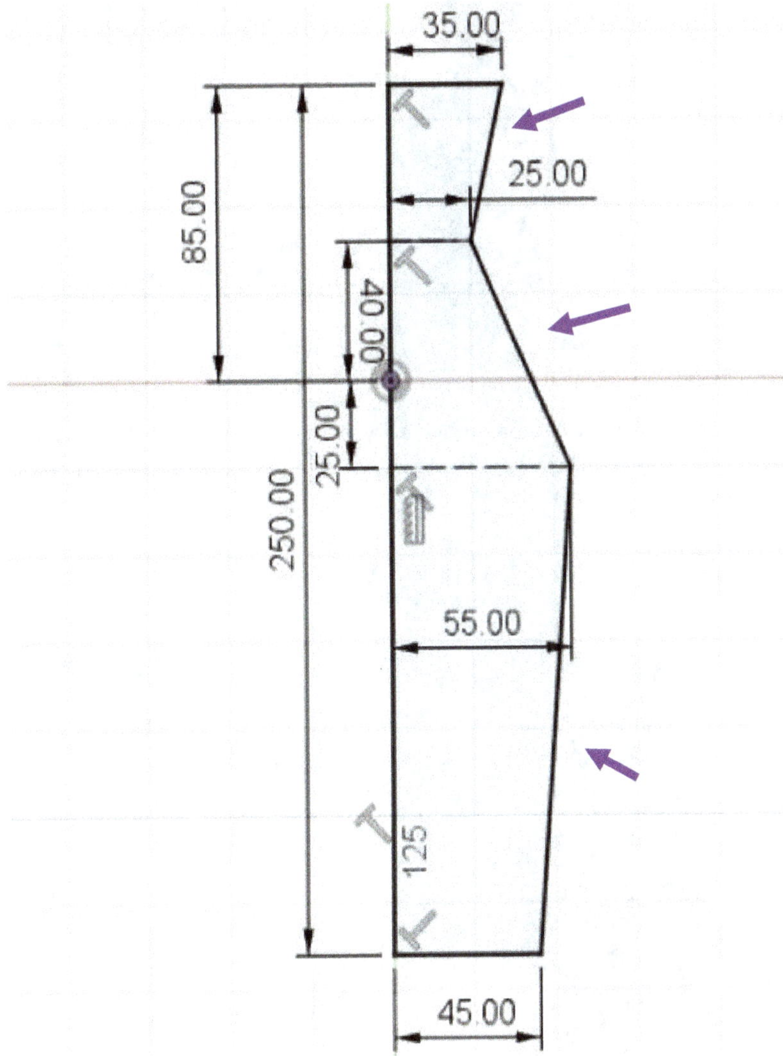

Then we can switch to 3D mode and create the vase using the "Revolve" command. To do this, we select the profile as usual, if that is not already selected, which is unlikely, and then the rotation axis, which in our case is the blue z-axis. Again we need 360 degrees for the rotation, and then we can confirm.

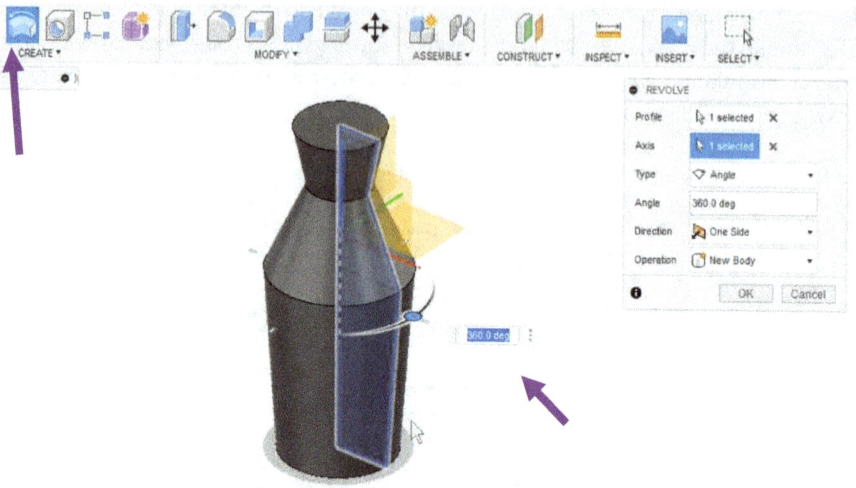

The basic body of the flower vase is now ready. Next, we hollow out the body by using the Shell command and clicking on the top surface of the vase. For the wall thickness, we can choose, for example, 3 mm.

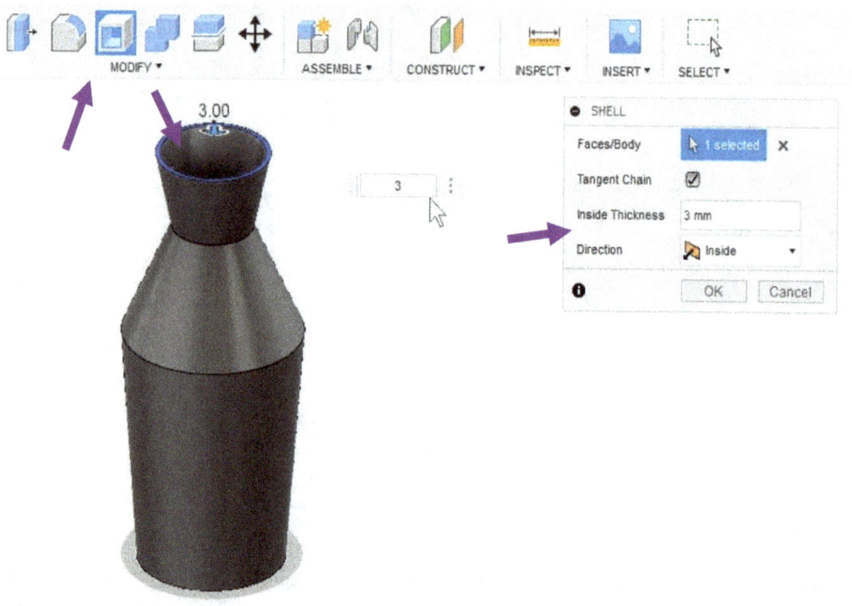

To improve the angular design a bit more, we add a fillet of 10 mm for the bottom edge.

For the three remaining edges, for example, we choose fillets of 1 mm.

As a final step, we would like to change the appearance of the flower vase. By right-clicking on the body in the part browser and selecting "Appearance", we can adjust the appearance to our liking.

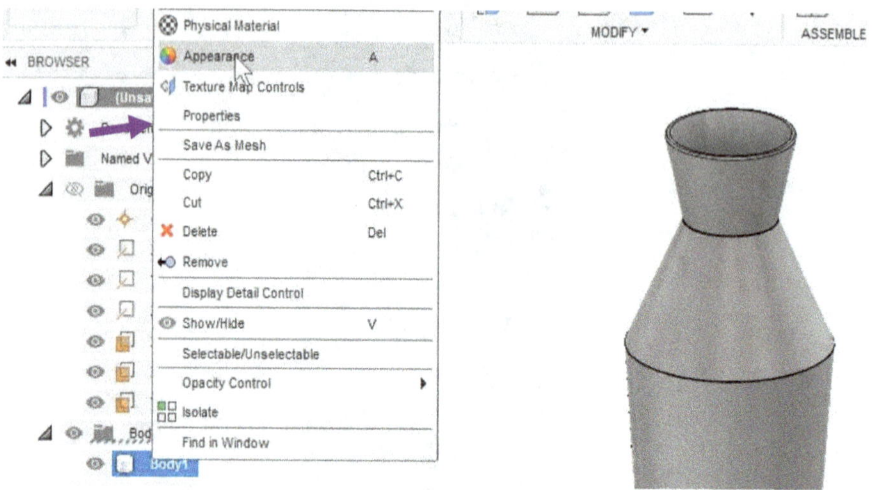

At the bottom, we can search for a suitable appearance in the Fusion 360 library. We can also use the search function if we already have a specific color or material in mind. For example, we could transfer the appearance of a sapphire to the vase with a click and drag motion.

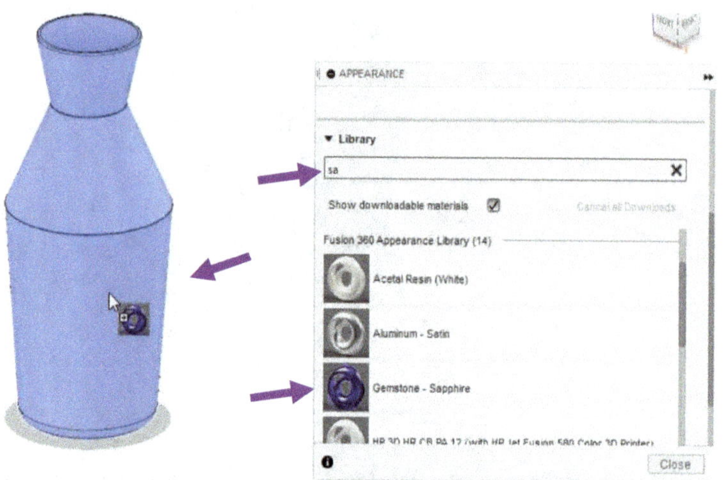

Let's get back to more difficult designs, such as a screwdriver and a wrench, in the next two projects before moving on to the second section.

6 Project 5: Slotted screwdriver

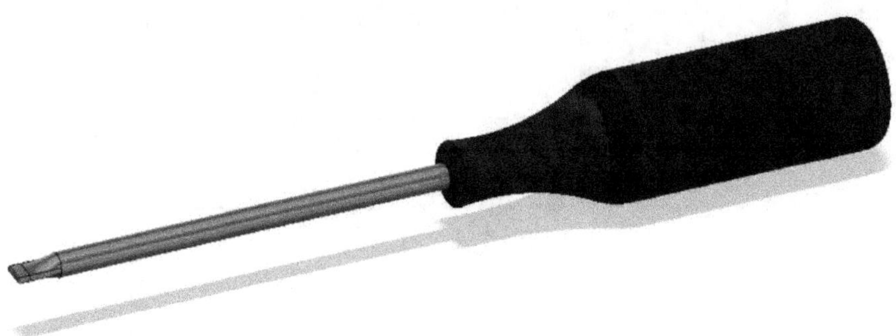

We start for the slotted screwdriver with the handle, which we will again create as a rotational part, as this will be easiest for the following geometry. To do this, we first create a 2D sketch again, e.g., on the x-z plane and draw a horizontal 110 mm long line, which we place symmetrically in our sketching environment with 55 mm distance to the center.

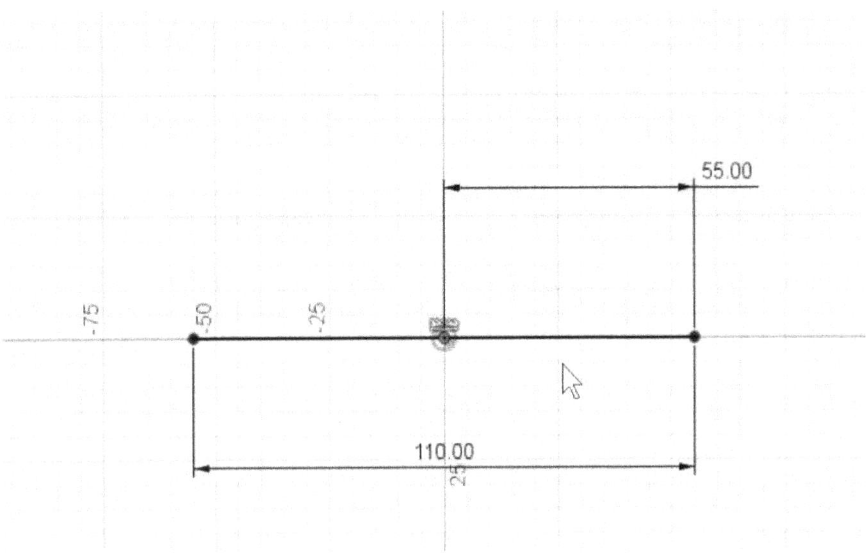

We also need a coincident link between the line and the origin to fully define the line. A 15 mm long vertical line and a 70 mm long horizontal line, connected to it, represent the first part of the handle for the screwdriver.

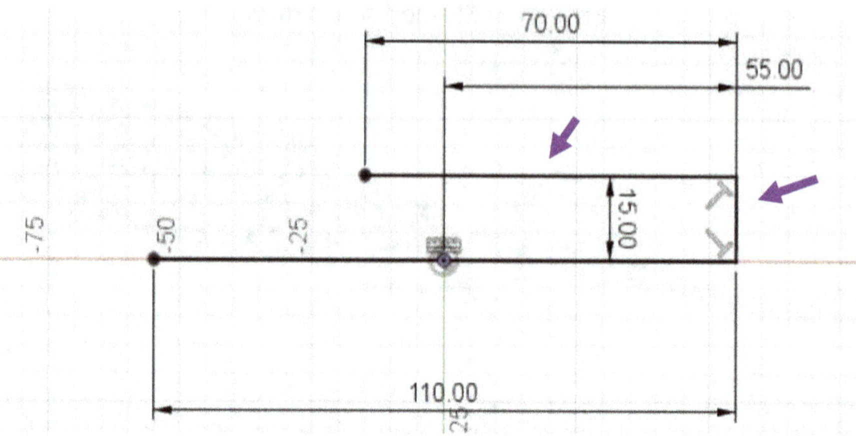

For the second part, we require an 8 mm vertical line and a 3-point arc connecting the previous profile. It should have a radius of, for example, 60 mm.

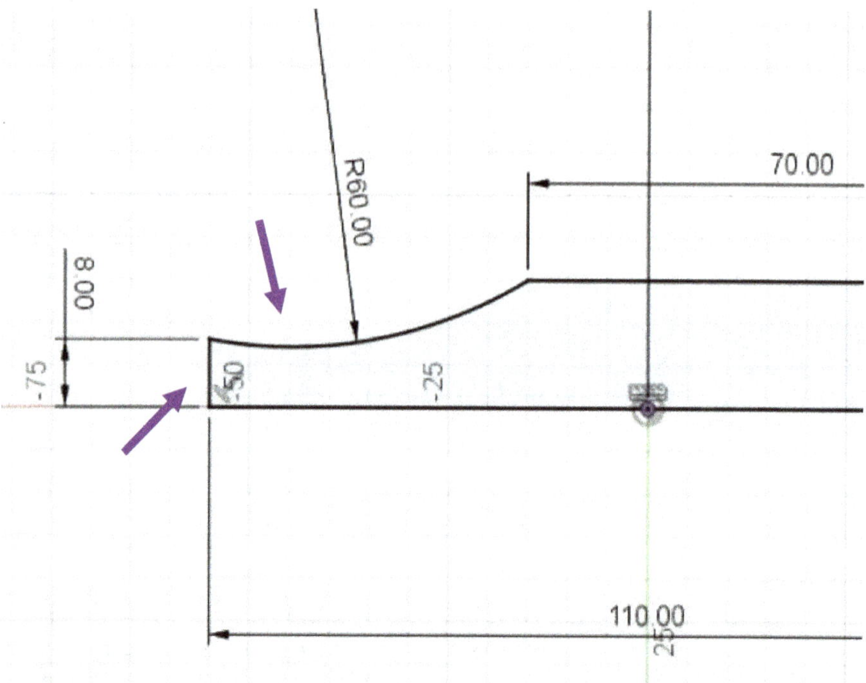

We will now also make fillets in this 2D sketch using the "Fillet" command. For the rear outer edge of the screwdriver handle, we will choose a radius of 5 mm.

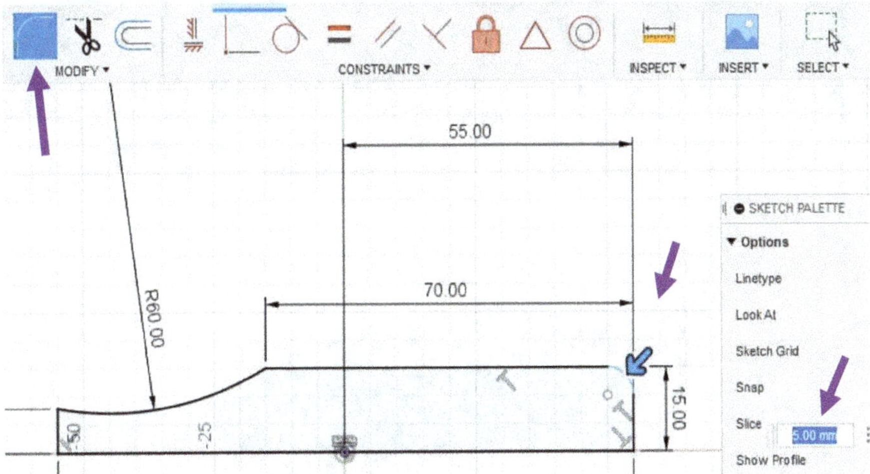

For the transitions in the front area, 15 mm and 2 mm.

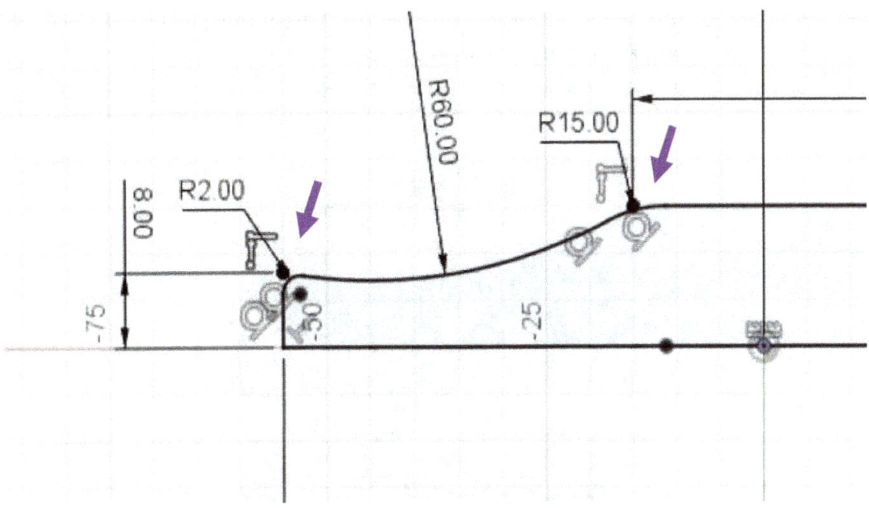

We will not draw the blade and the blade tip in this 2D sketch. If you want, you can also add the blade tip to this sketch, but we will add it as an extrusion in a moment. First, however, we need to switch to 3D mode and rotate the profile for the handle in this case around the red x-axis using the "Revolve" command.

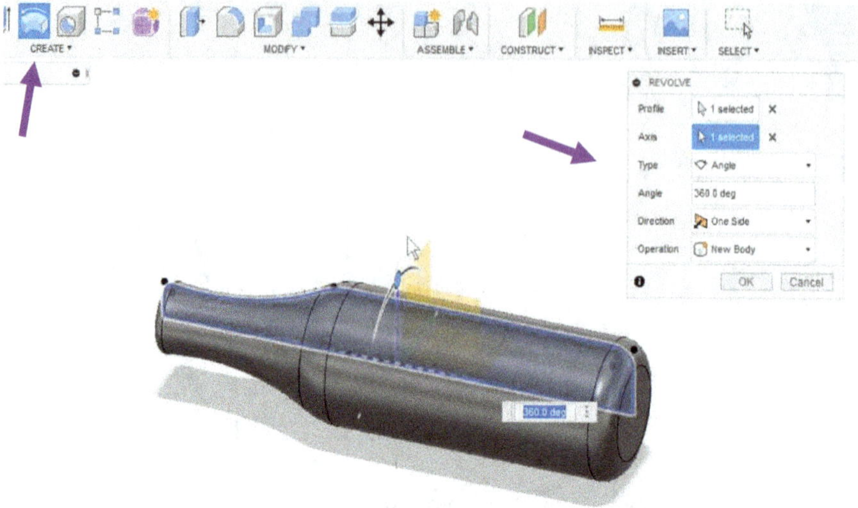

As mentioned earlier, we will now add the blade of the screwdriver, which we will sketch onto the front face of the handle. We simply need a circle in the center for the linear extrusion. The diameter should be, for example, 6 mm.

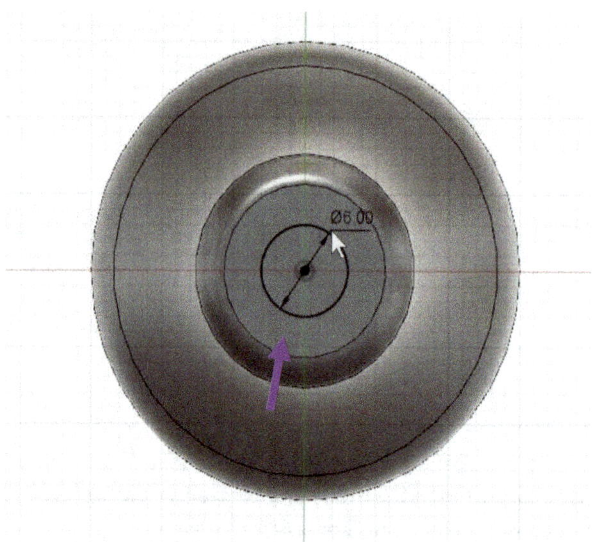

We then extrude the profile by 100 mm and obtain our screwdriver blade in this way. In the settings, however, we select "New Body" in this case so that we can then later design the blade independently of the handle.

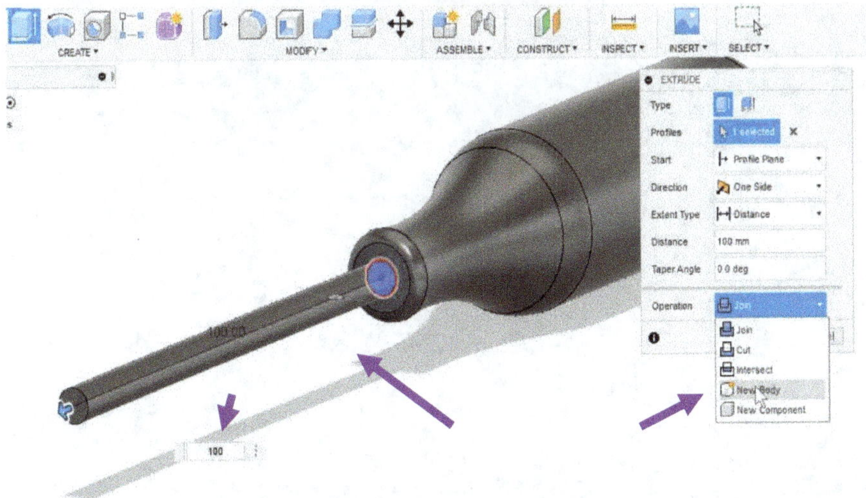

In reality, these two parts are also made of different materials. Now the bit or the blade tip in the front area is still missing. We want to create a slotted screwdriver, so we will use the "Loft" command to create the bit. To do this, we first create a parallel plane to the face of the tip using the "Offset Plane" command. We need a distance of 8 mm.

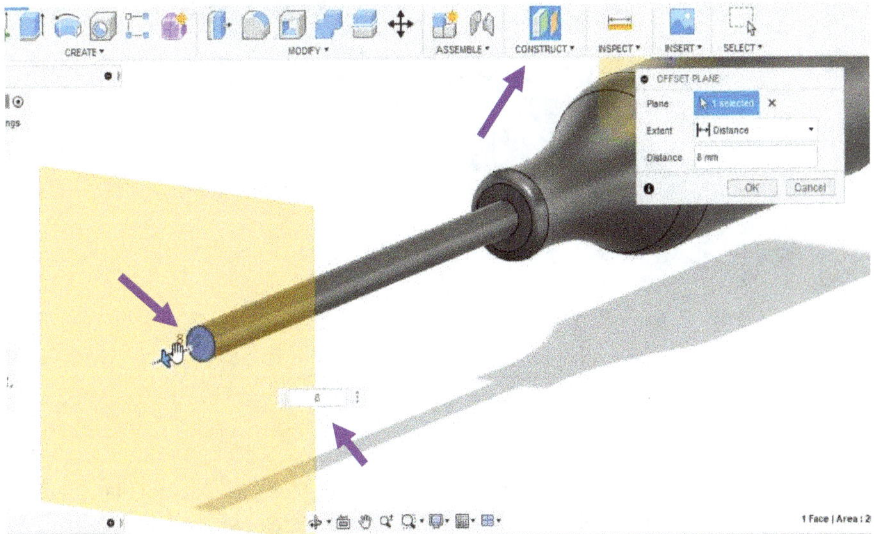

On this plane, we can now draw the rectangular profile of the bit. We use a center rectangle for this, whose corners we fix with coincident mates on the circle of the screwdriver blade. Finally, we have to dimension the width of the rectangle, e.g., with 1.5 mm.

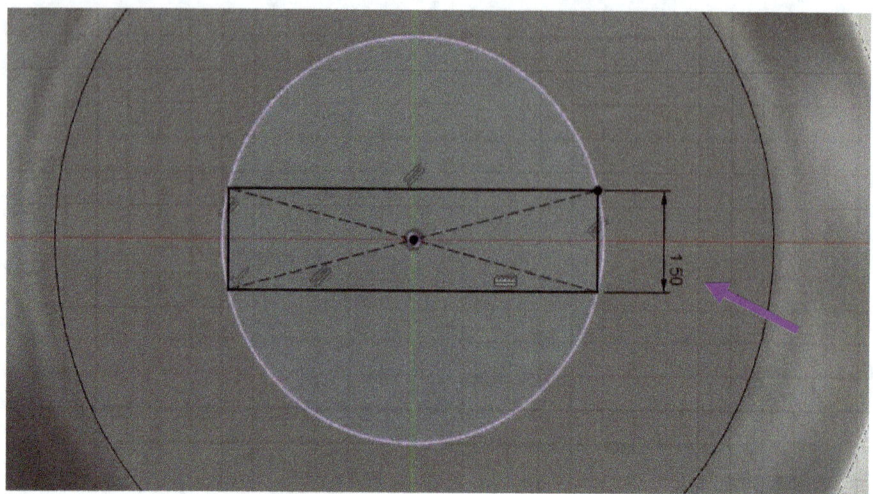

After we have closed the 2D sketch, we can now use the "Loft" command to connect the sketched profile with the circular geometry of the screwdriver blade. This will look like this:

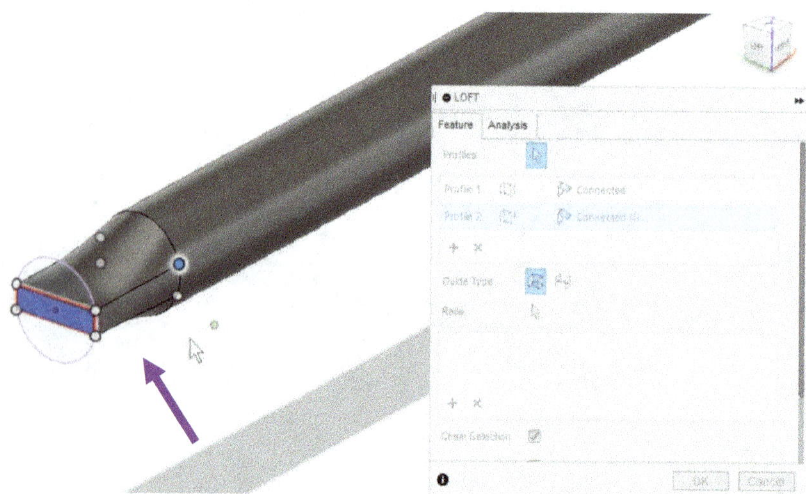

We get a nice transition between the blade and the bit. Since the rectangular shape of the bit is now a bit too small at the front to be able to screw with it, we now have to extend it a bit. To do this, we simply sketch a congruent rectangle and then extrude it 3 mm.

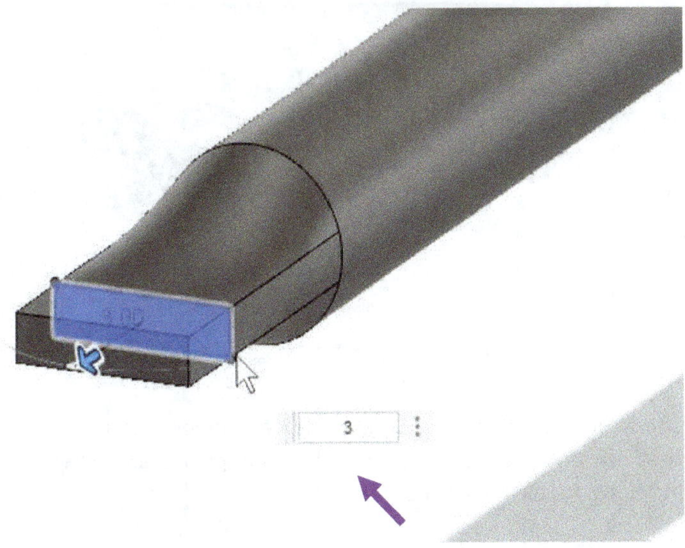

Now it looks better. We add a 0.3 mm chamfer to each of the two horizontal edges of the bit using the "Chamfer" command.

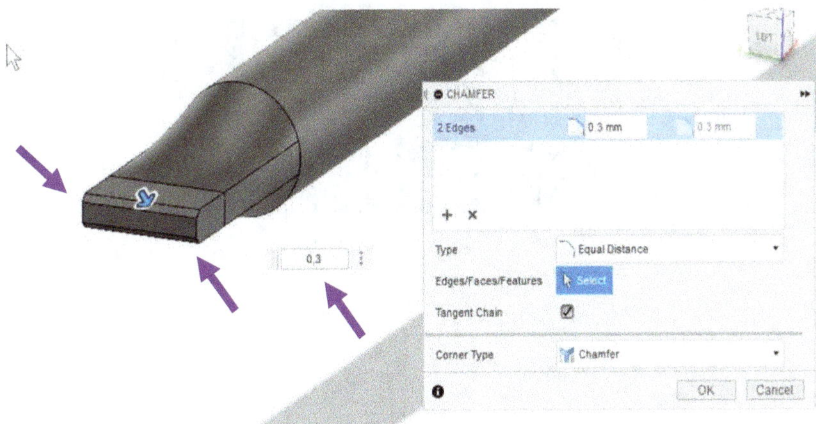

To finish the project, we would like to improve the appearance a bit. For example, we want the handle to be made of a wood material. To accomplish this, we'll search "Appearance" for a noble wood, such as walnut, and drag the appearance onto the body of the handle with the mouse. Great!

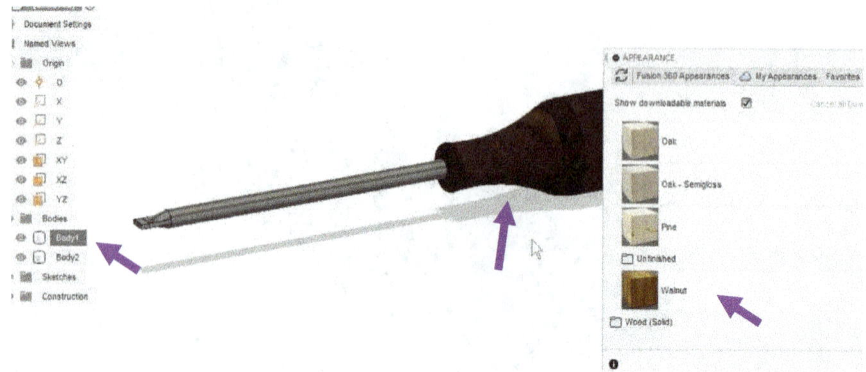

The screwdriver is ready! Fittingly, the next project continues with a wrench. Be sure to stick with it, more exciting and difficult design projects will follow in the second part, including, for example, a ball bearing.

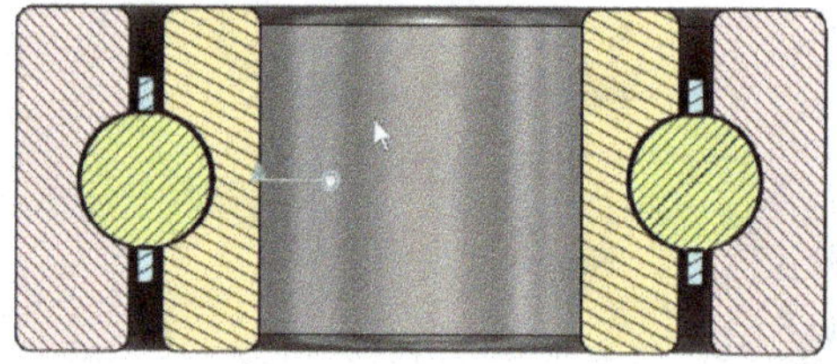

7 Project 6: Wrench (open-end wrench)

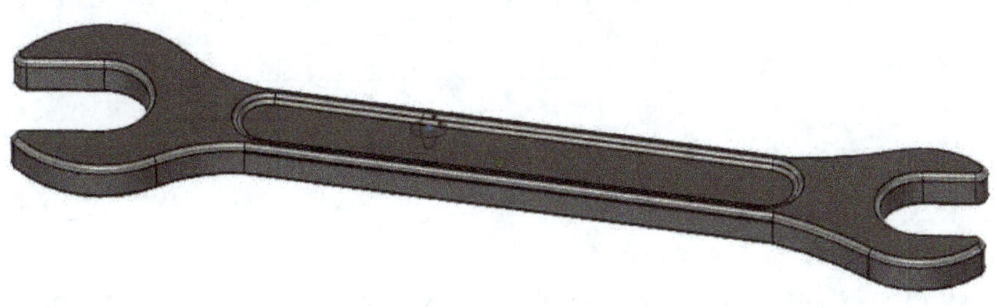

How can we best create this wrench? If we take a closer look at the geometry of the wrench, some of you may already recognize that it makes sense to start with a circular geometry in the left and right areas and to build the middle area of the wrench with arcs and connecting lines. The other details will follow later. So let's first sketch two circles on the x-y plane. The left circle should have a diameter of 35 mm and the right one a diameter of 28 mm. We set the left circle with 67 mm distance to the origin and the right one with 65 mm. Horizontal mates with the origin are still missing for the complete definition.

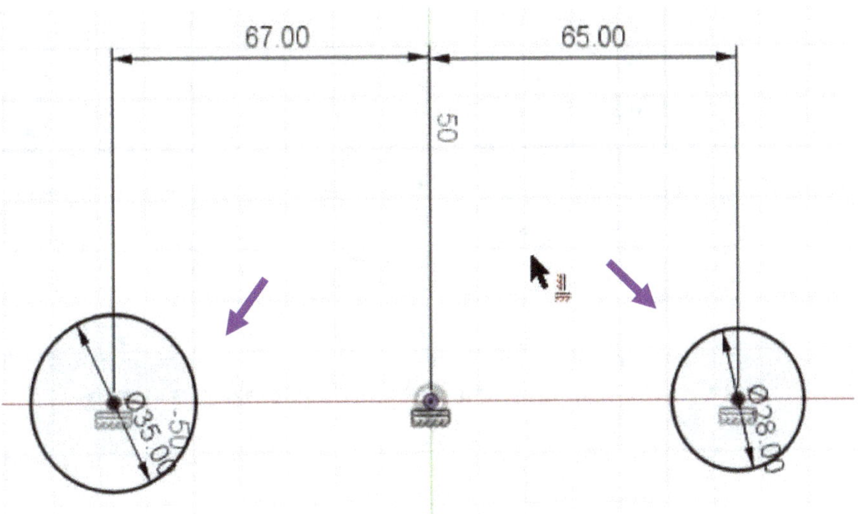

Now we create the middle area. To do this, we first draw a line 85 mm long with a distance of 7.5 mm and 42.5 mm from the origin. In the lower area, we draw an identical line and apply the Equal relationship so that the two lines are equal. We also add dimensions in x and y direction to the origin again.

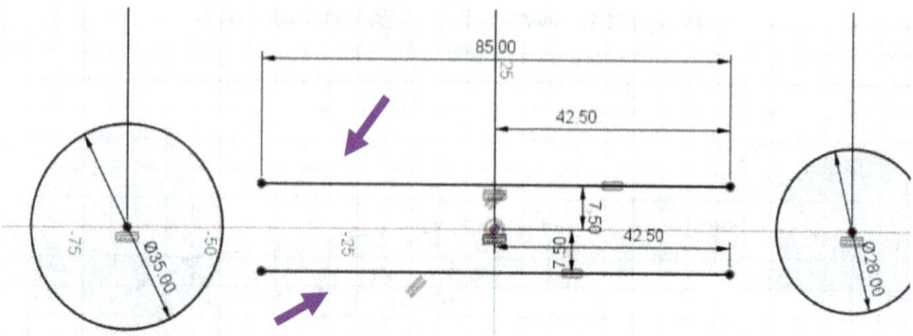

Then we draw two 3-point arcs in the left transition area, whose start and end points are to start and end on the circle and the end point of the line, respectively. We define a radius of 25 mm for these arcs.

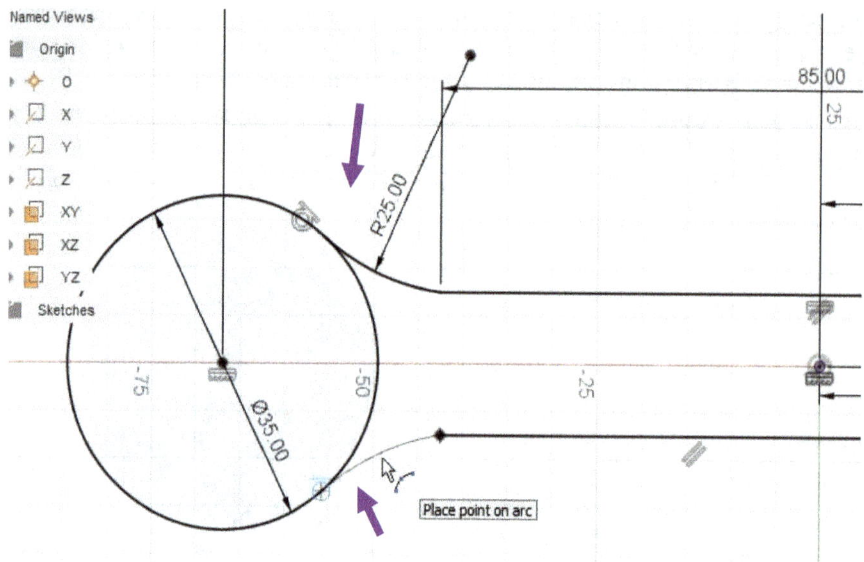

We do the same in the transition area of the right side. However, the radius here should be 65 mm in each case. Then we can remove the excess arc segments of the two circles with the "Trim" tool.

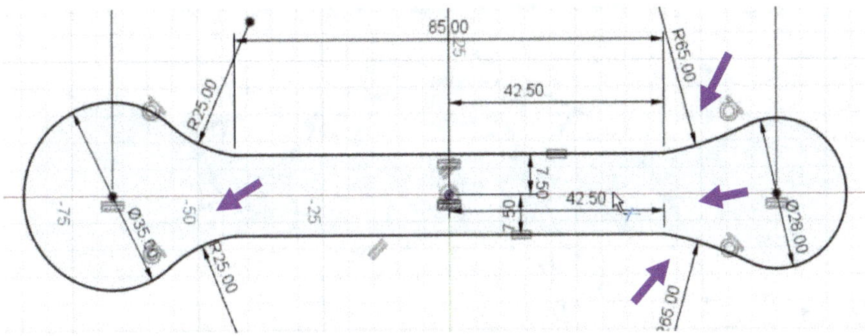

We now turn our attention to the two cutouts that enable the actual function of the wrench. We would like to integrate these into the sketch at the same time to save us one or more work steps. Let's start again in the left area. This geometry is also easiest to sketch with the help of a circle, which we place in the center and do not dimension for the time being.

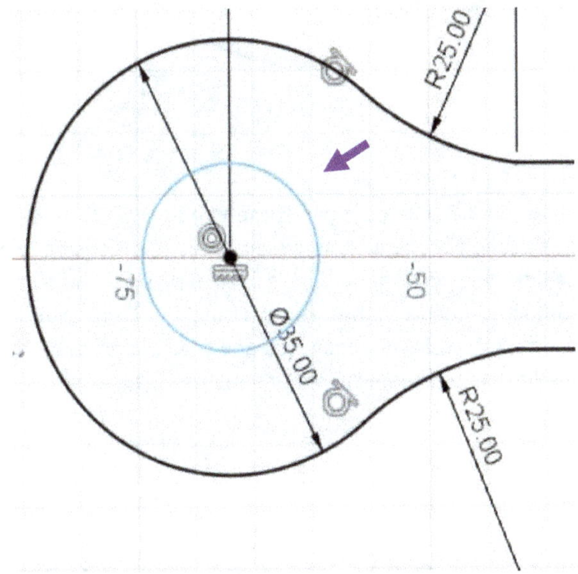

We then add a line that should start at the outer circle and be tangential to the inner circle just drawn. Make sure that the tangential relationship, recognizable by the small symbol, is created. Otherwise, just add it manually. We also need such a line in the lower area. We then set the two lines in parallel dependence with a relationship.

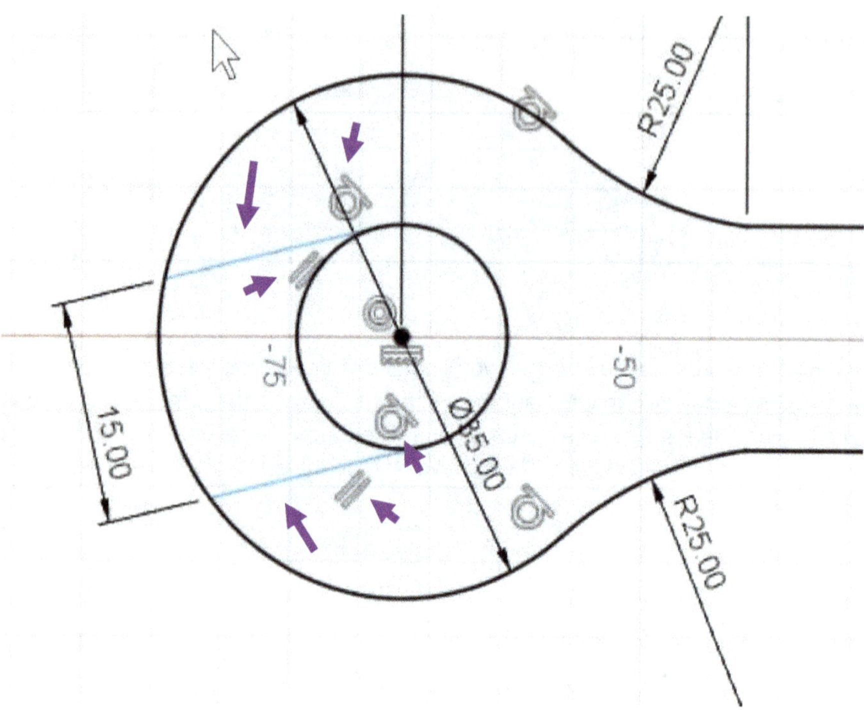

Now we dimension the distance between these two lines as 15 mm. So, we get a 15 mm wrench on this side. For real use, however, the dimensions or tolerances from a table book or the Internet should definitely be used here, since there must still be some space between the screw head and the wrench. Using the "Trim" command, we remove the superfluous arc segment in the inner area and then add a horizontal auxiliary line, which we will need for dimensioning in a moment.

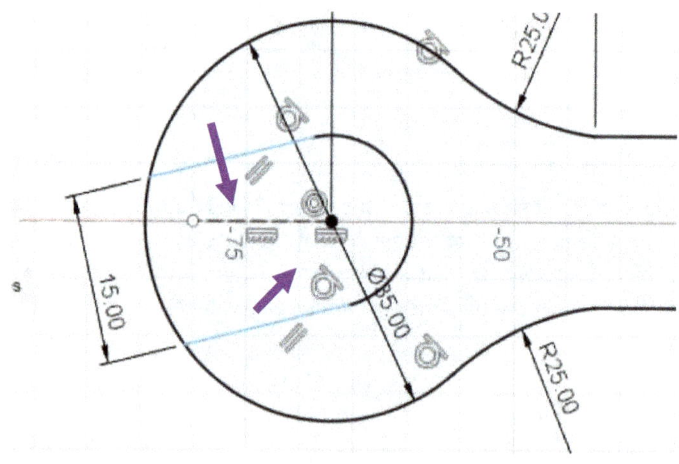

We now dimension the angle between the top line and the auxiliary line, since the opening should sit at a slight angle. We choose an angle of 10 degrees. Then the sketch is completely defined again. Finally, we remove the second superfluous arc segment of the outer circle and get the desired opening.

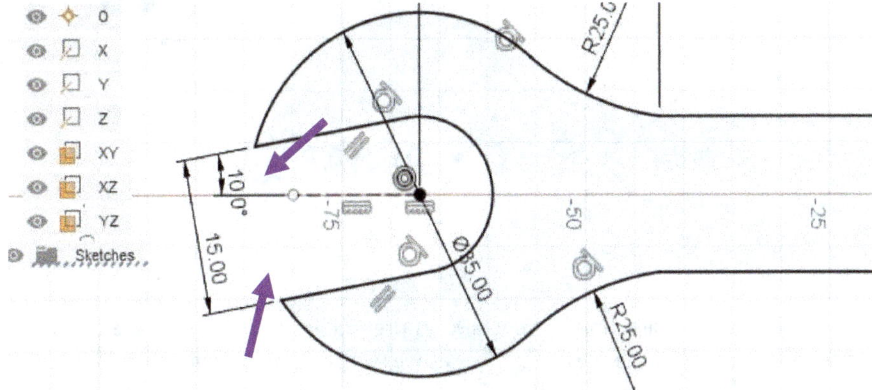

We do the same procedure on the other side. Only the dimensions are different, we want a 13 wrench size. Feel free to try it out for yourself! As said, the procedure is identical.

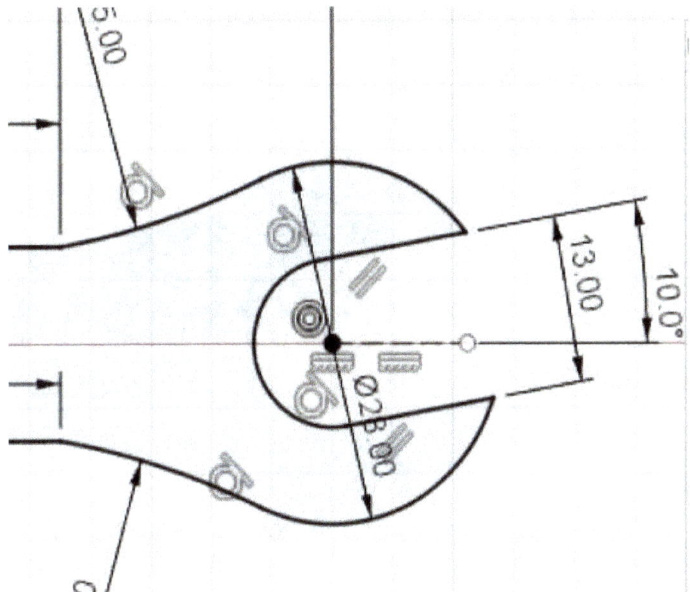

Perfect! The profile is then ready, and we can finish the 2D sketch. We now simply extrude the profile 3 mm with symmetrical direction.

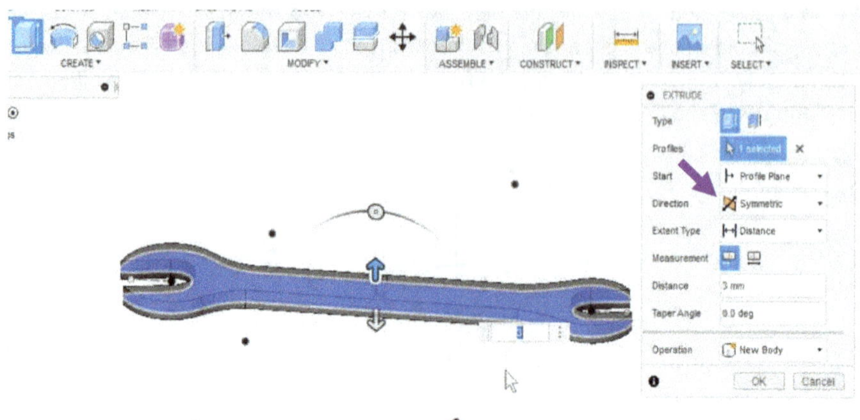

Why a symmetrical direction? This is always preferable for parts that are to have a plane in the center of the part because – as we will see in a moment – we can mirror symmetrical features more easily. Furthermore, for assembly, it sometimes offers advantages to have a plane in the middle instead of on the top or bottom of the part. We now want to add another indentation or embossing in the center area. To do this, we sketch a center elongated hole on the top or bottom surface.

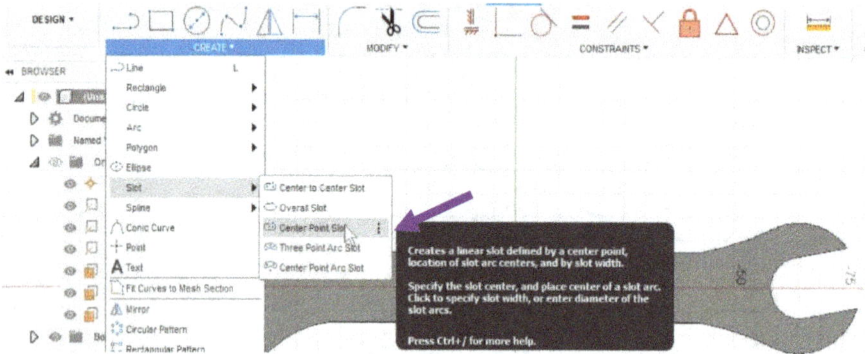

The length of the oblong hole should be 80 mm and the width should be 10 mm.

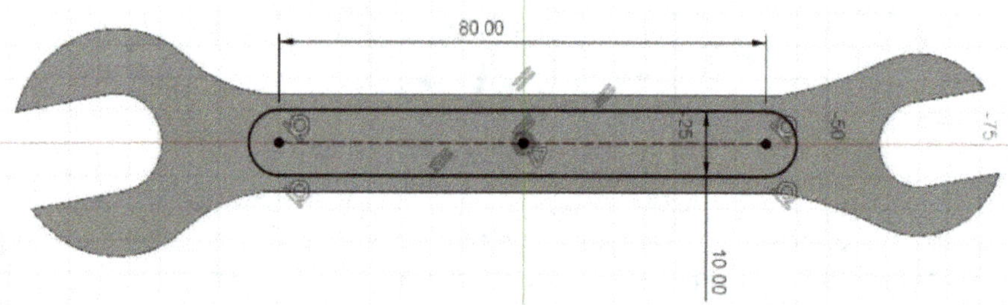

We then emboss this profile with "Extrude" alternatively also with "Emboss / Deboss" -1 mm into the component.

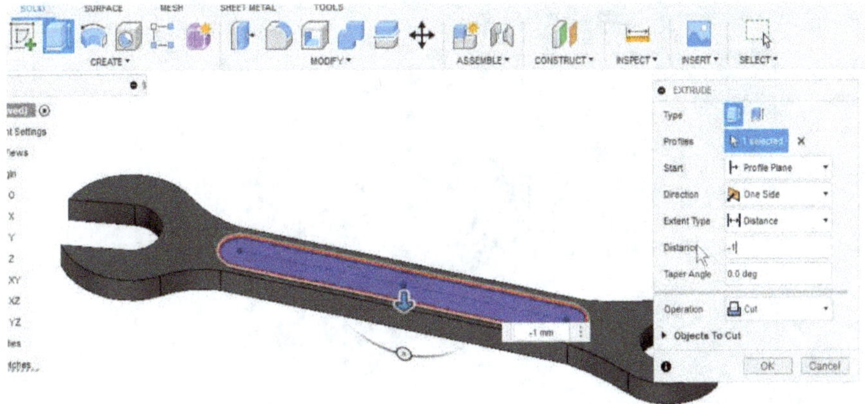

Since the part is symmetrical about the x-y plane, we can now easily create this indentation for the other side using the Mirror command. Select the feature in the Timeline, as well as the command in the "Create" menu, and then change the selection to "Mirror Plane" in the settings.

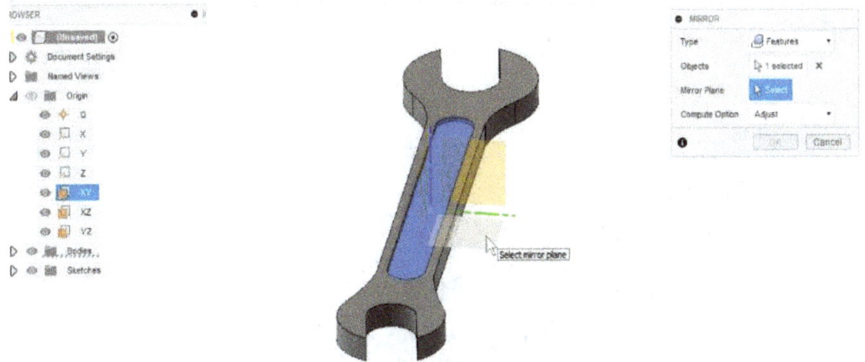

Now we can simply select the x-y plane, since it is already correctly placed in the center – remember? Confirm with "Ok"! We then round off the four edges of the receptacles of the wrench with, e.g., 2 mm. You can select further edges by holding down the CTRL key.

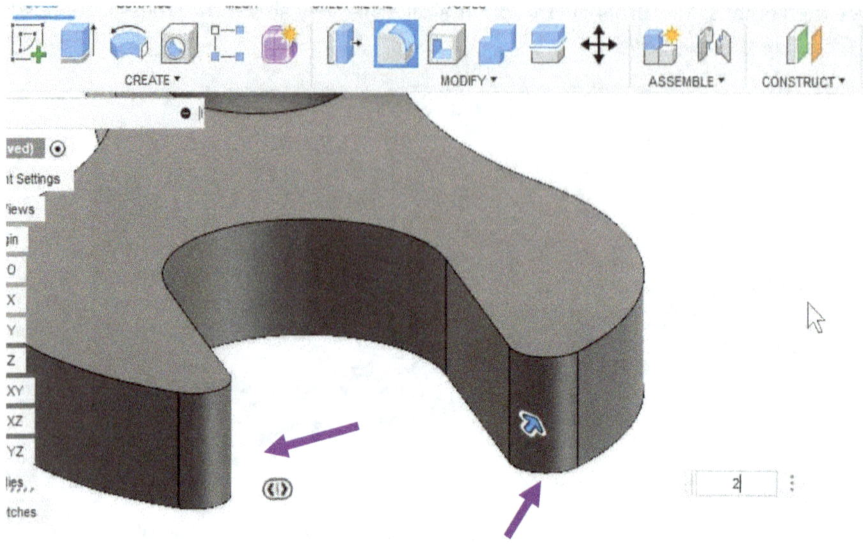

Finally, we select all the faces and round the edges with a 1 mm radius using the Fillet function.

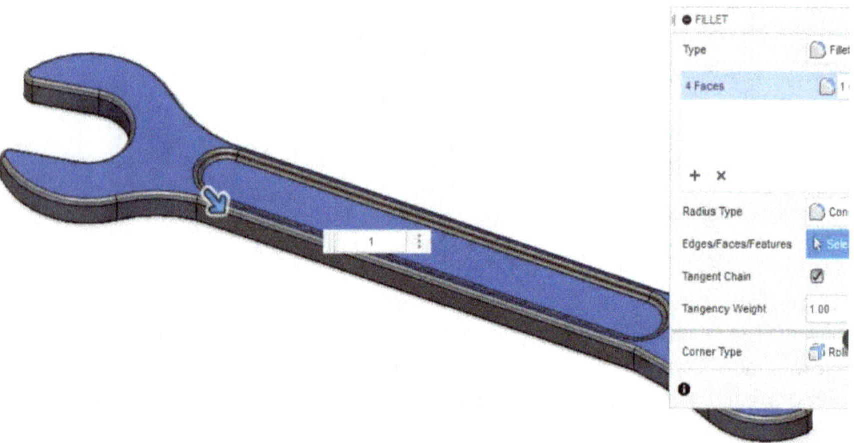

Excellent! We are done! Those were the easy design projects. Hopefully, you have enjoyed it so far. But of course, this is not the end of the story. In fact, more complex design projects will now follow in the second section. Let's go on!

Section II: Medium difficulty design projects

8 Project 7: Ball bearing

Welcome back. The first design project from this section will be a ball bearing. More specifically, a single row deep groove ball bearing, which is one of the best known and most commonly used ball bearings. The ball bearing consists of four components. We will create these one by one. We need an outer ring, an inner ring, as well as balls and, as the last component, a so-called ball cage, which ensures that the balls remain in the correct position.

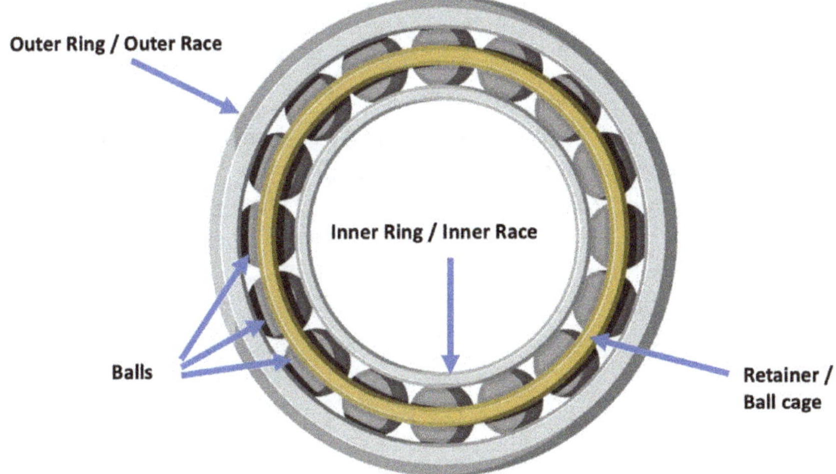

We will start with the first component, the outer ring of the ball bearing. Likewise, we will create this with the help of a rotation, for which we again need a 2D sketch first. We start on the x-y plane with the cross-section of the outer ring. To do this, we first draw a 20 mm wide and 7 mm high rectangle in the plane.

After moving it a bit more centered and deeper, we dimensioned the horizontal distance from one of the side edges to the origin with 10 mm, so that the rectangle sits centered. We dimensioned the upper edge with 25 mm to the origin to finally define it completely.

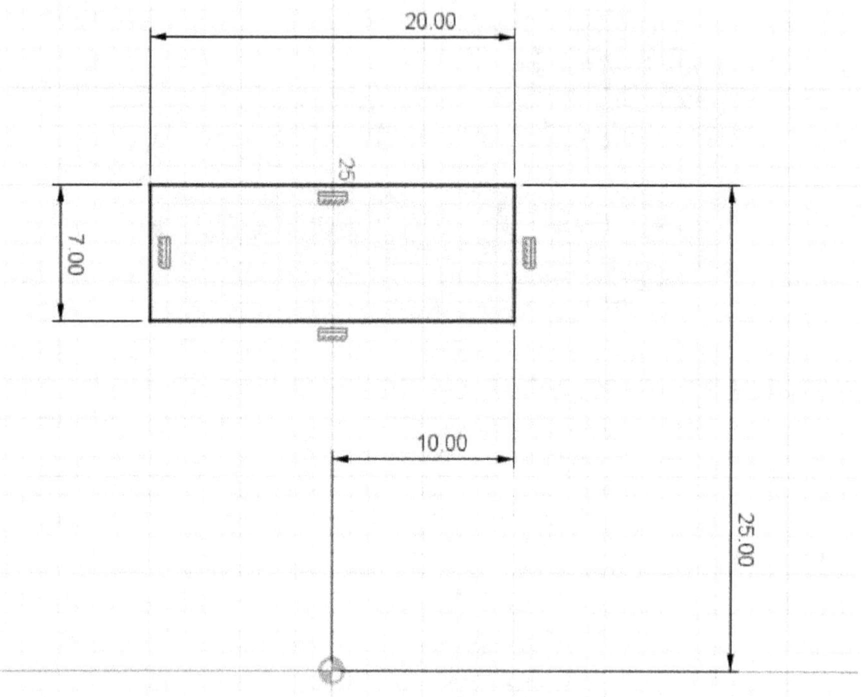

Then we need to create the raceway for the balls. To achieve this, we use a circle that we place as shown and provide with a diameter of 8 mm. We dimension the distance between the center of the circle and the top edge of the rectangle as 7.8 mm.

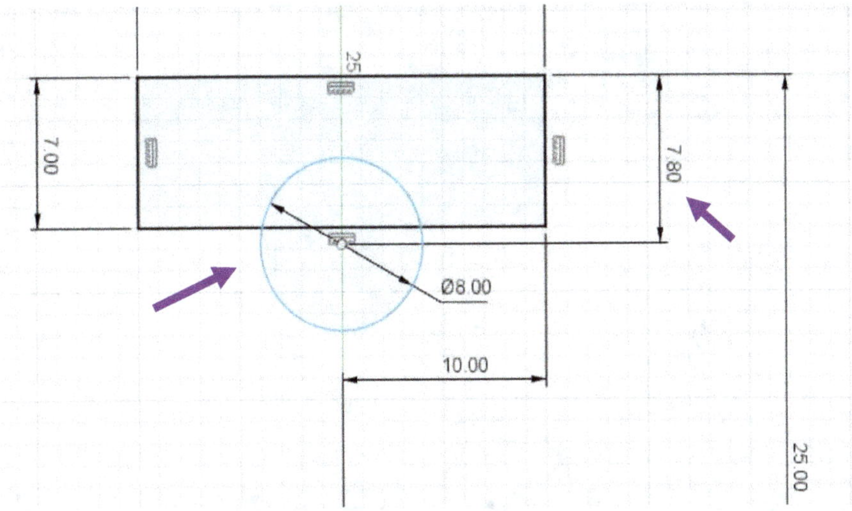

Then we remove the two superfluous profile sections as shown and link the circle center still with a vertical condition to the origin.

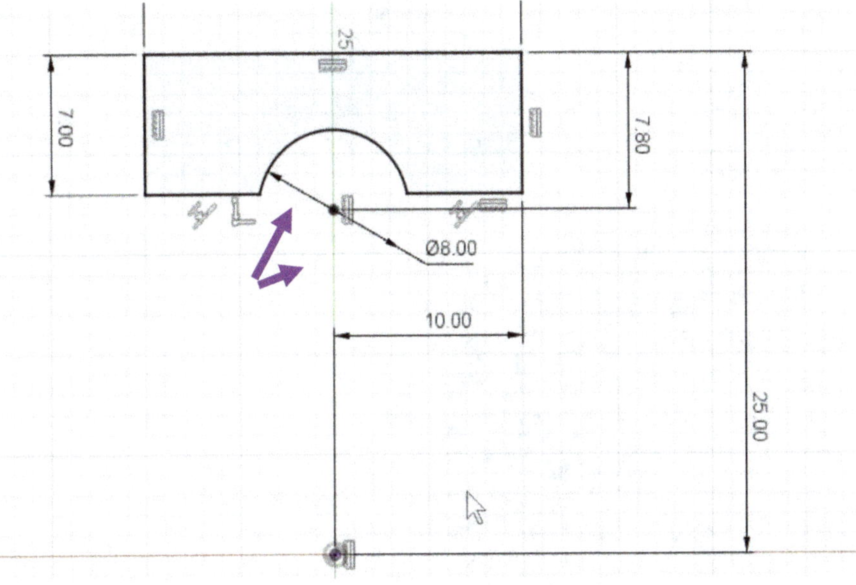

As a last step, we can also create fillets for the edges of the part. To do this, we create fillets with a radius of 1 mm already in the 2D area using the "Fillet" command.

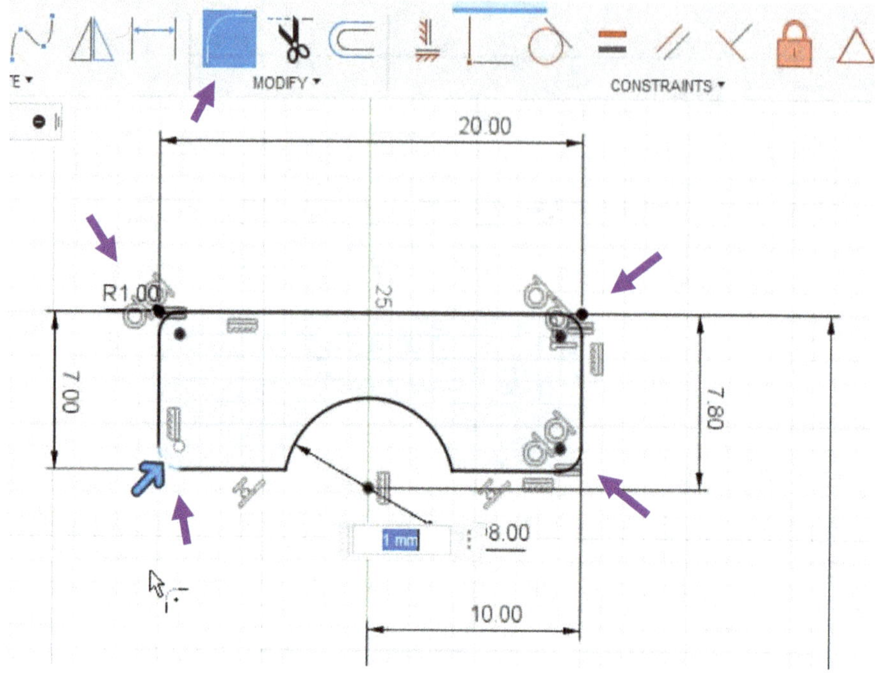

Then the cross-section profile of the outer ring is ready and can be rotated around the red x-axis in 3D mode using the "Revolve" command in this case. We need a full 360-degree rotation.

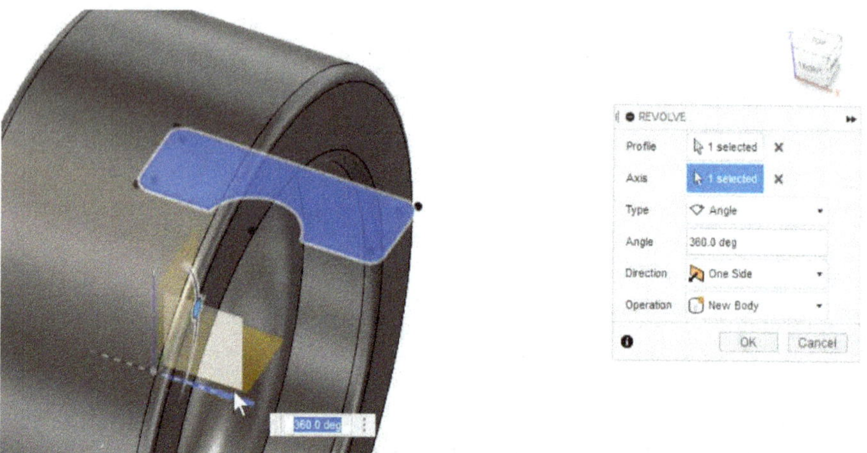

For the second part of the ball bearing, which is to be the inner ring, we must first create a new component, since this is an independent part that will be assembled later. We select the "New Component" command, which can be found in the "Assemble" menu.

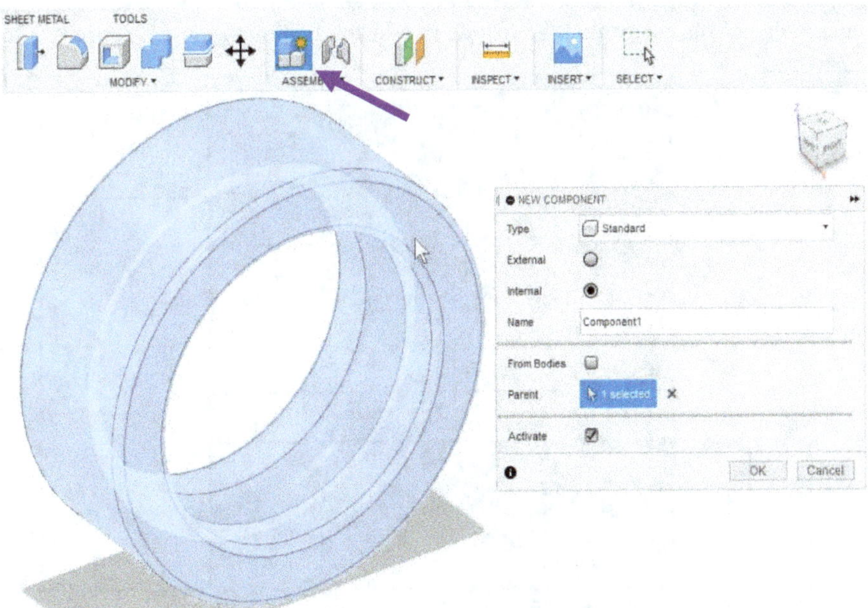

On the x-y plane of this new component, we will then sketch a cross-section geometry analogous to the previous part, which we will then again transform into a 3D component using "Revolve". To do this, we will start again with a rectangle that we dimension 20 mm wide and 6 mm high. We define the vertical distance from the origin to the lower edge of the rectangle as 16 mm, and the horizontal distance between one of the side edges to the origin as 10 mm.

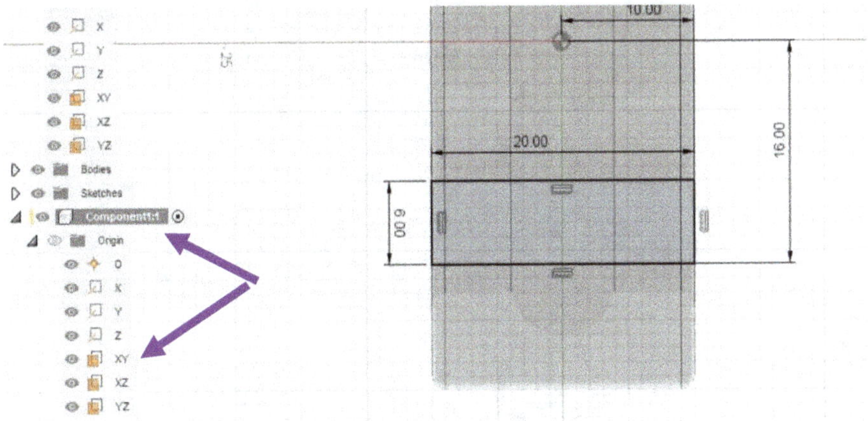

Then we sketch the raceway for the balls. We do this, as was already the case with the outer ring, with the help of a circle. The diameter must be identical, i.e., 8 mm. A vertical link to the origin and a distance of 6.8 mm between the center of the circle and the upper edge of the rectangle then follow, so that the two raceways are concentric to each other.

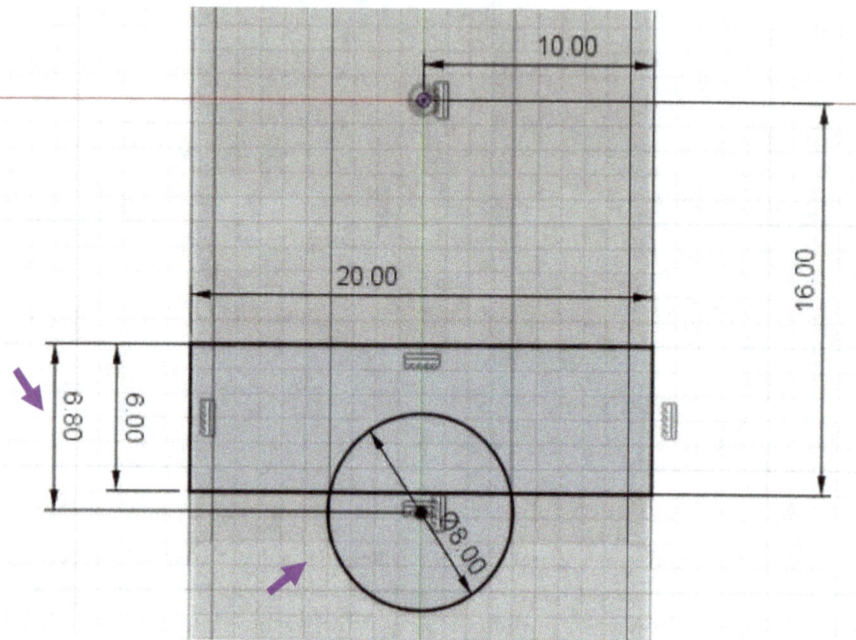

In the last two steps for the profile, we again remove the superfluous profile sections as shown and create 1 mm fillets for the edges of the inner ball bearing ring.

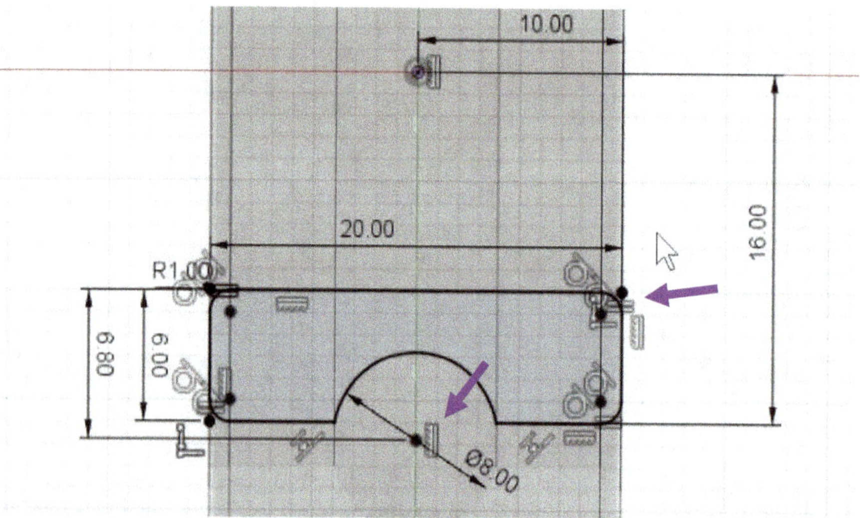

In 3D mode, we can then perform a 360-degree rotation.

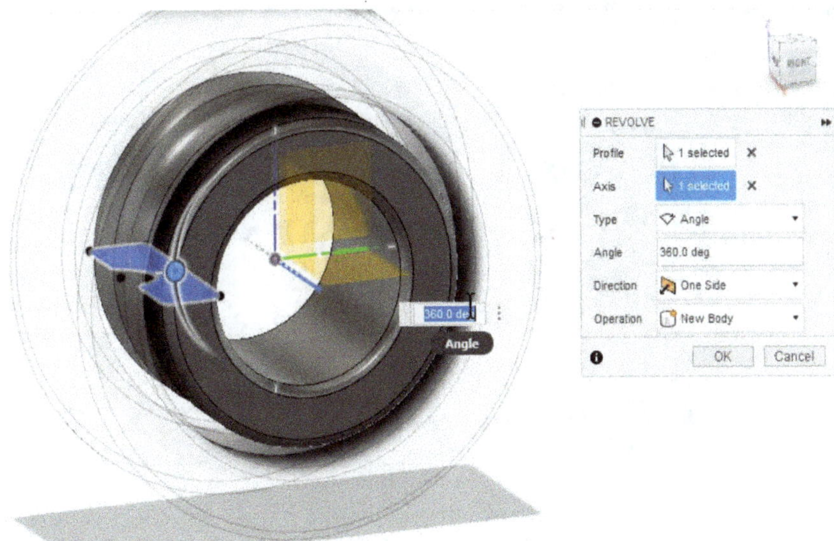

For the next part, the ball cage, we will create a new component, since this part is again an independent component. We'll sketch on the y-z plane of the new component this time, since we won't be rotating the part, but using an extrusion to create it. We simply need to sketch two circles, each of which should start at the center point and have a diameter of 33 mm and 35 mm respectively.

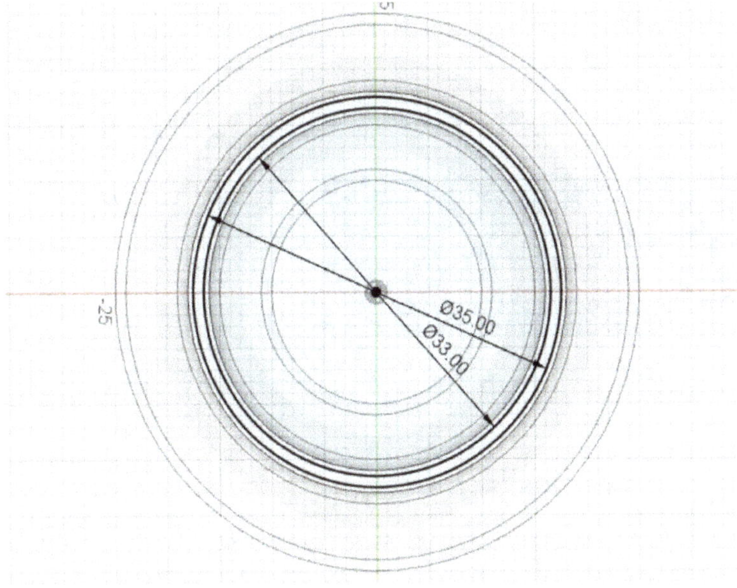

Then we can make a symmetrical extrusion with 6 mm spacing.

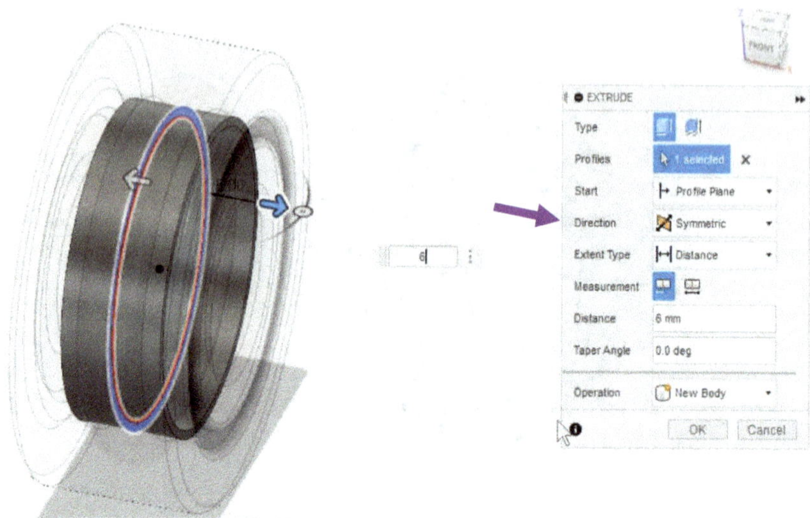

Now we have to add holes where the balls will sit later. To do this, we use the "Hole" command. First, however, we hide the other two bodies to be able to work better. Then we place a 7.8 mm hole with 2 mm depth in the upper center of the ball cage. We need a simple hole, with no thread and no point angle. After we have placed the hole exactly in the center, we can confirm with "Ok".

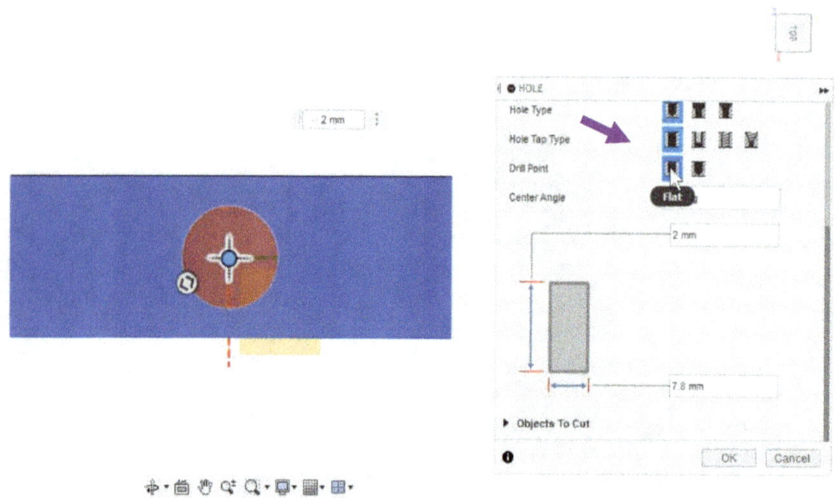

To create all further holes, we again use the already known function "Circular Pattern".

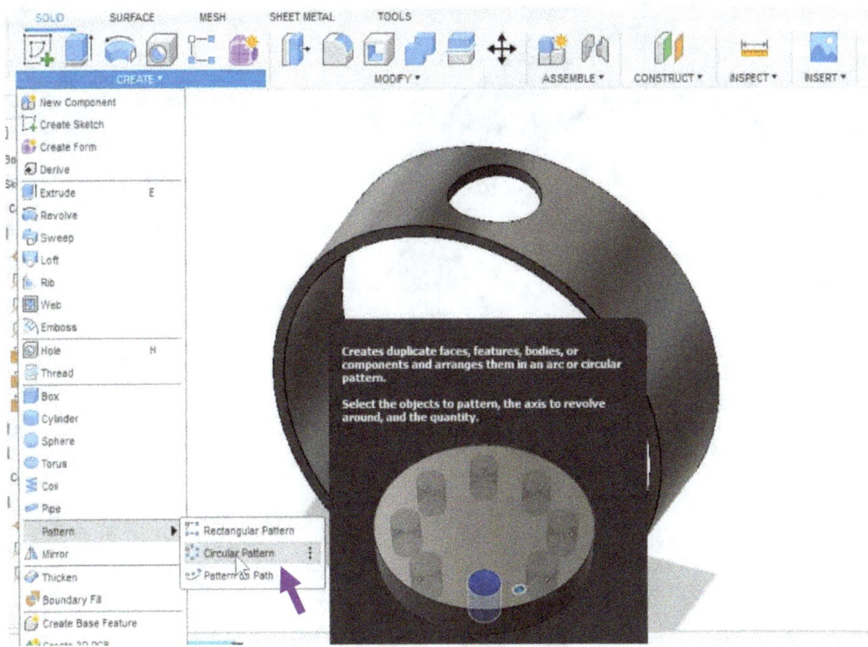

In the command settings at "Type" first switch to "Features", change the selection to "Objects" and then select the bore feature in the timeline.

In the next step, switch to "Axis" and select the x-axis. For example, we need 10 holes because we want 10 balls in our ball bearing.

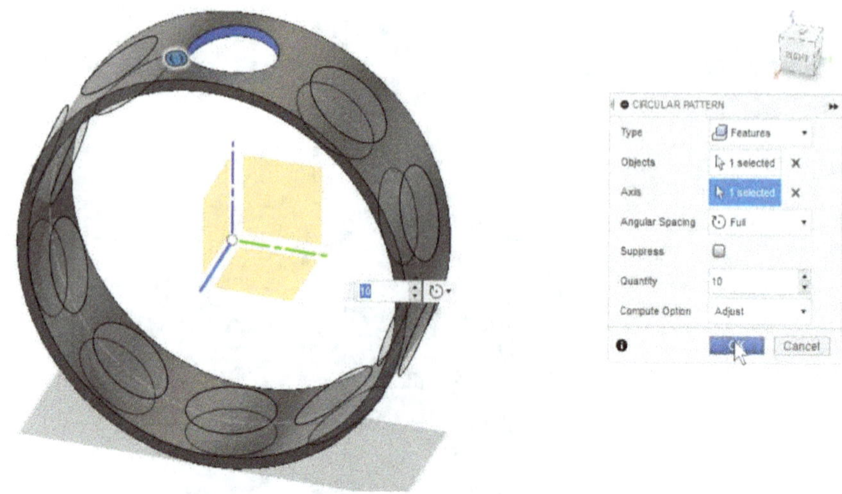

Then the ball cage is done.

Before we can link all the components together using joints, we want to create the last component, the sphere. We will then simply copy this sphere 10 times. To do this, we will use the predefined element "Sphere" from the "Create" menu.

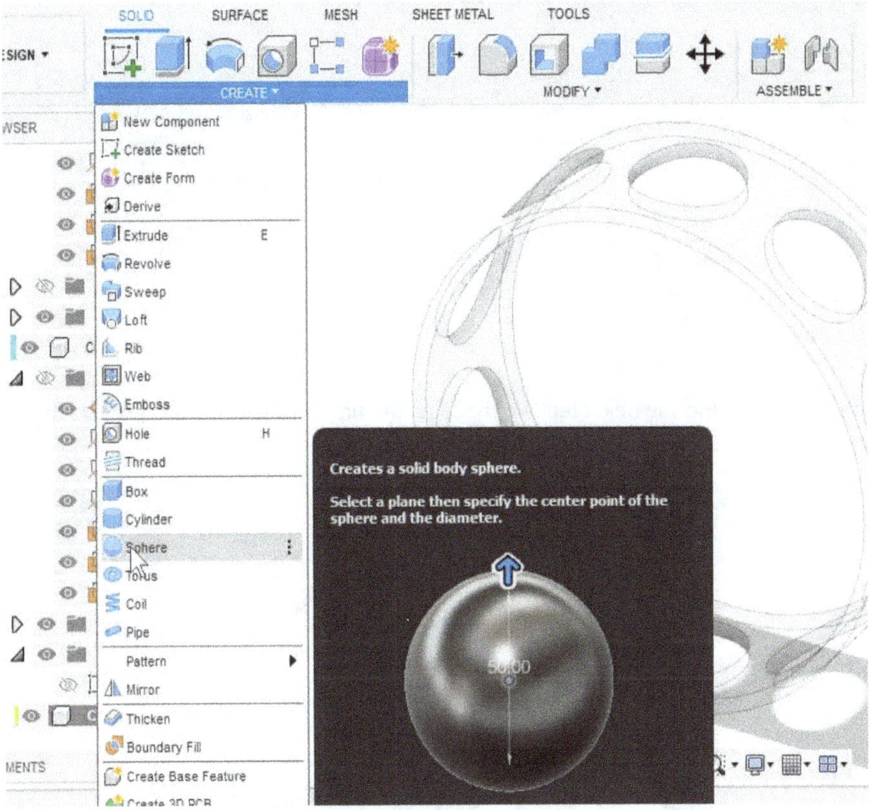

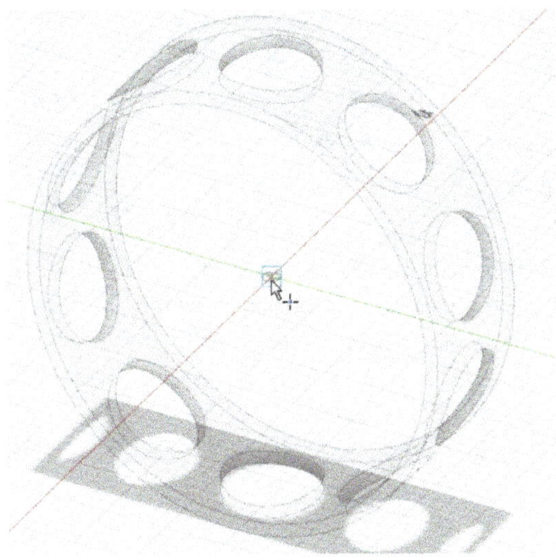

After selecting the command, we need to draw on a plane the diameter of the sphere, for example, on the x-y plane, a diameter of 8 mm.

It's that simple! In the next step, we then link the first ball to the ball cage. To achieve this, we use the "Joint" command from the "Assemble" menu.

As we already know from the Fusion Beginner course, we now have to determine a joint origin on each of the two components to be linked and specify the type of joint. For the sphere, we simply place the origin of the joint at the center point.

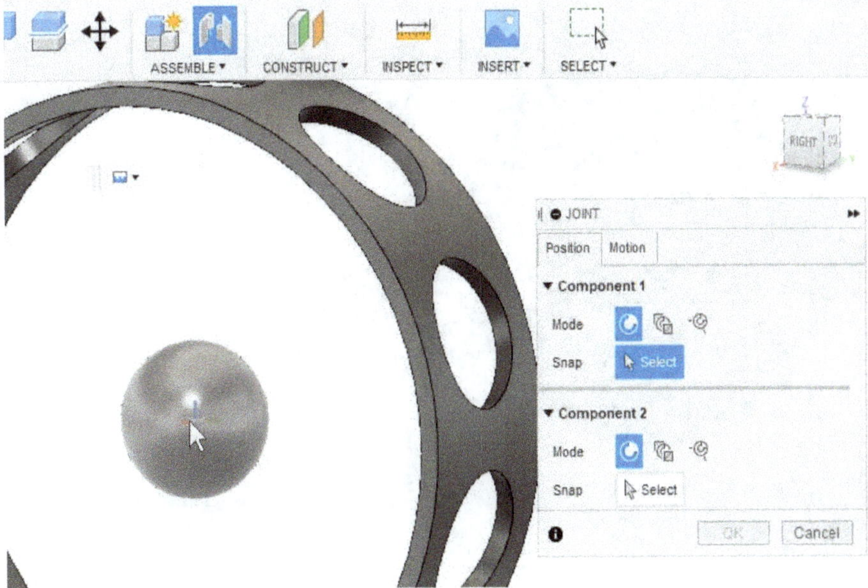

For the ball cage, we choose the top center of one of the holes as the joint origin.

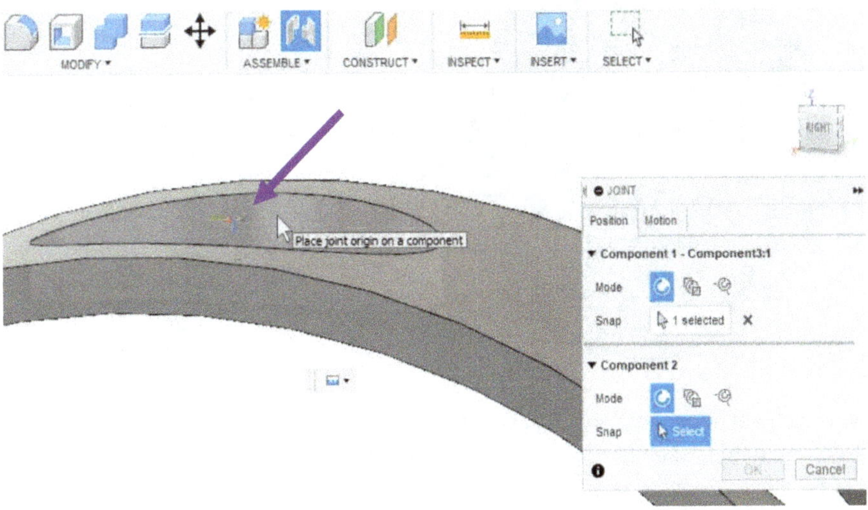

To make sure that the ball is exactly centered, we now need to add a 0.5 mm offset in the z-direction in the settings.

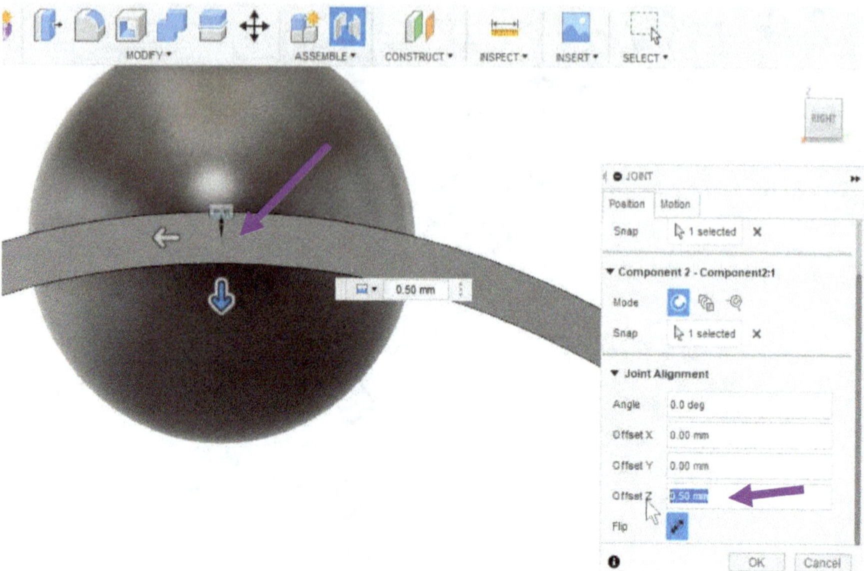

We select "Revolute" or "Ball" as the joint type.

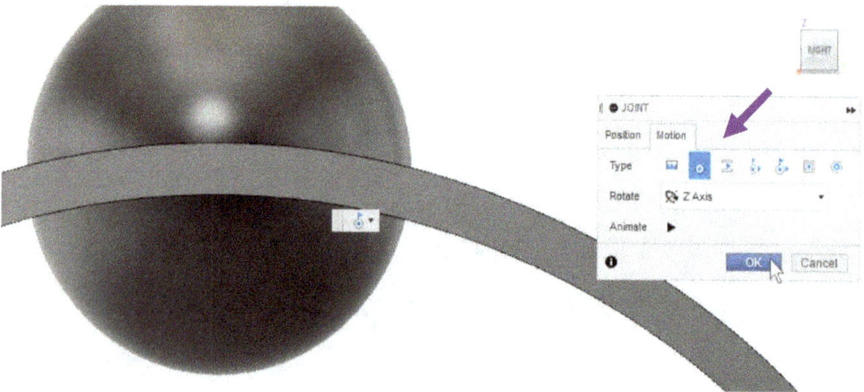

Now we need nine more spheres. We create them by simply copying the first sphere. To place them in the right position, we use the "Circular Pattern" command again. As "Type" we first have to select "Components" in the settings. Then we select the sphere in the part browser with "Objects" and after we have changed to axis in the settings, we select the red x-axis. Logically, we need 10 spheres.

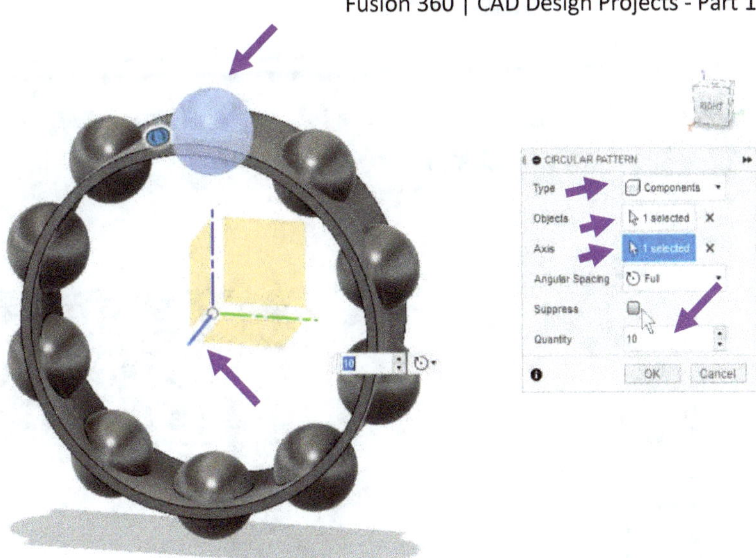

Unfortunately, although these balls are now in the correct position, they are not yet linked, i.e., we can still move them in the design space.

Now, so that we don't have to create a joint manually for each sphere, we use a new command called "Rigid Group", which is located in the "Assemble" menu. With this command, we can fix the relative position of the spheres as a group.

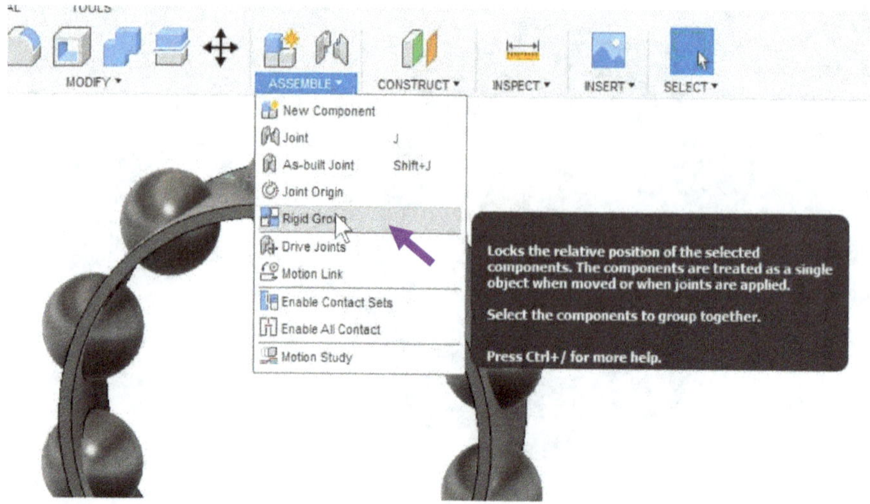

To do this, we just need to select all the balls, including the ball that already has a joint, and confirm with "Ok".

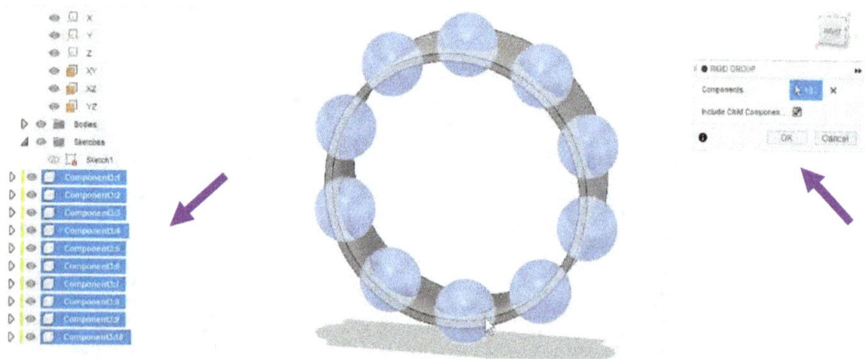

Now the balls are firmly fixed. To be able to carry out all other linkages, we show the outer and inner ball bearing rings again by clicking on the eye symbols in the part browser. We then create a joint between the two ball bearing rings by placing the joint origin in the center of each component. This may require some patience to get the proper point – the center point.

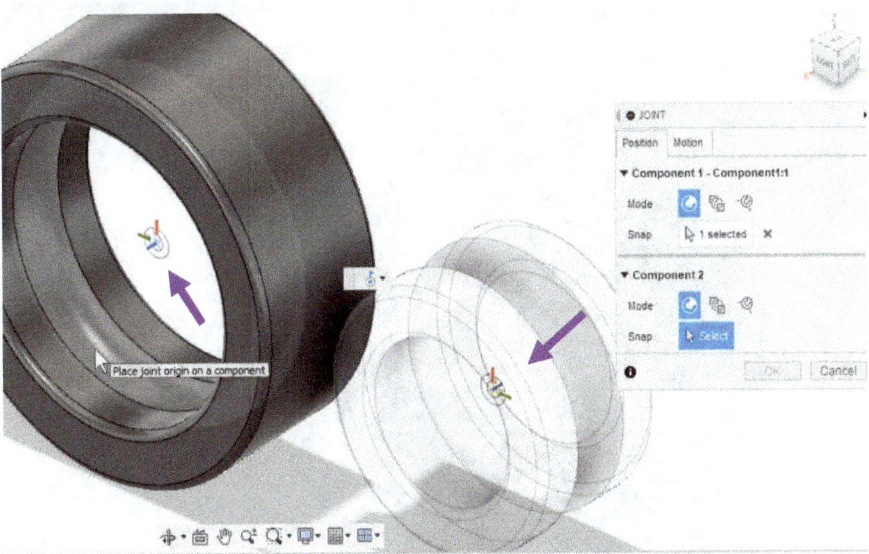

We select "Revolute" as the type of joint. Finally, we link the ball cage including the balls with the two ball bearing rings. To achieve this, we proceed in the same way as before. Place the joint origins in the center points and select "Revolute" as the joint type.

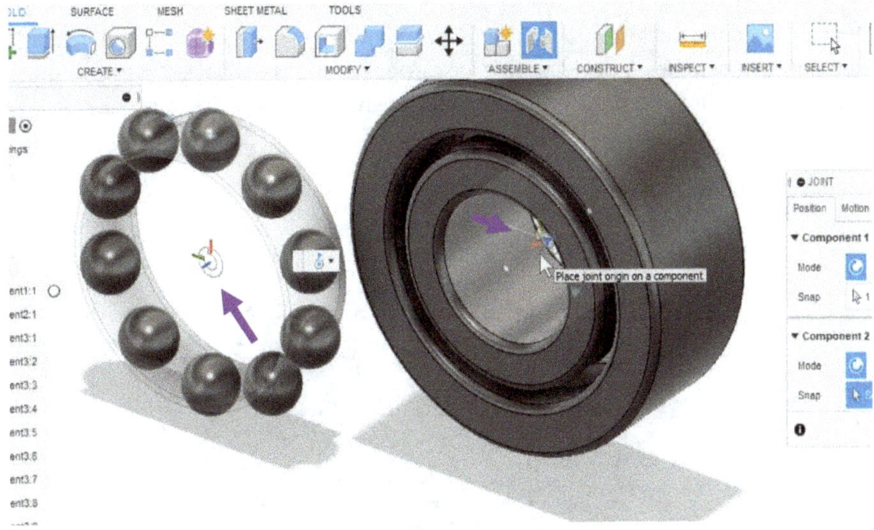

The ball bearing is ready! Super job! To see a bit more, we can create a section view so that we can also look inside. We do this with "Section Analysis" from the "Inspect" menu.

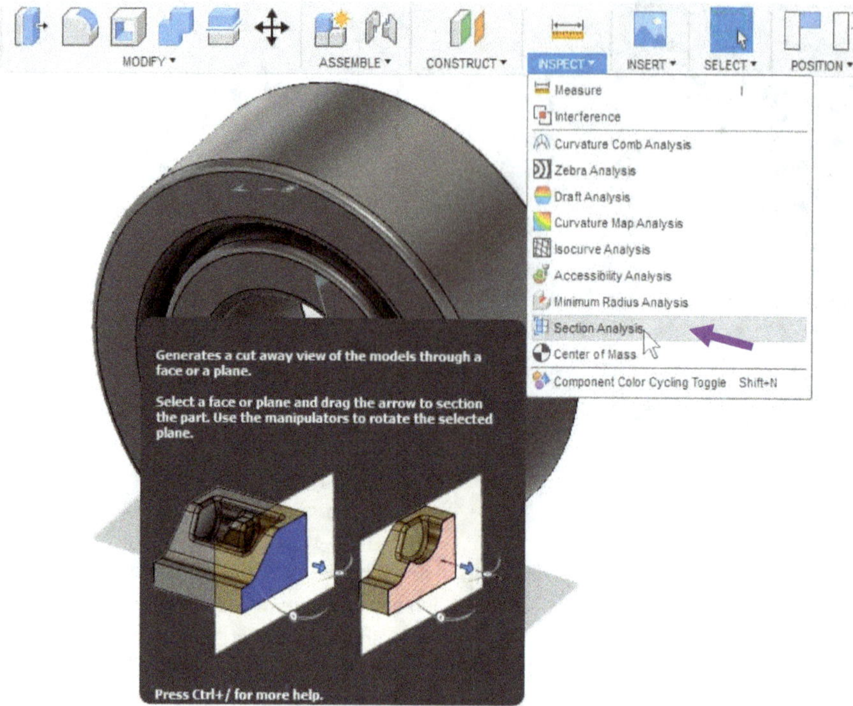

We then need to select the plane in which we want to intersect the component, in this case, for example, the x-y plane, so that we can look into it from above. If we now rotate the inner ring, we can see the balls moving through the bearing. Great, isn't it?

Alternatively or additionally, we can also influence the display of the outer ring by right-clicking on the body in the part browser and "Opacity Control" to be able to look inside.

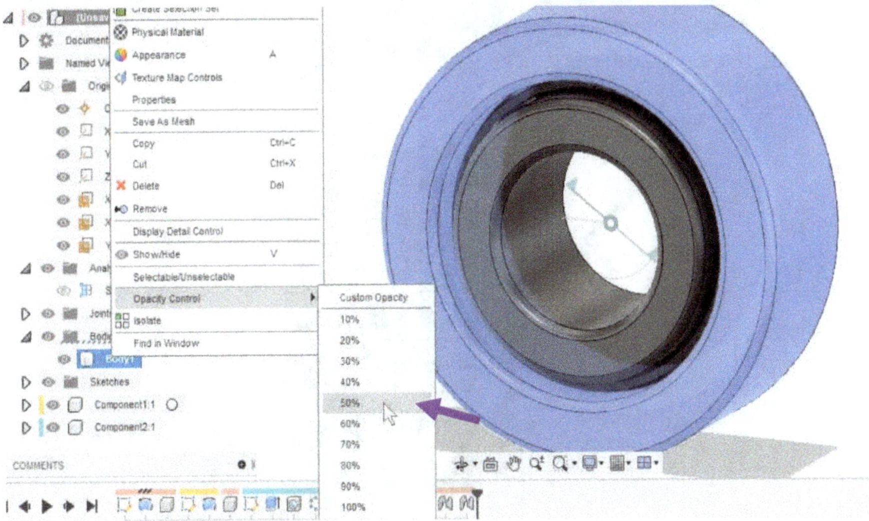

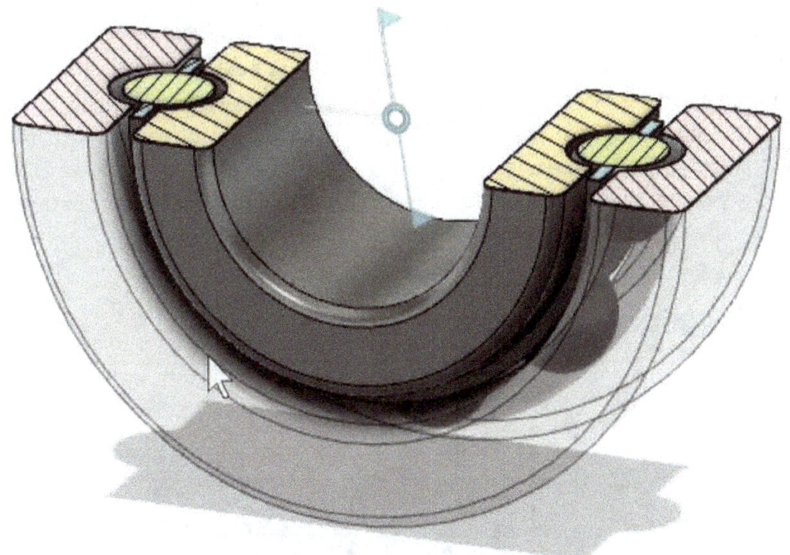

The next design project will be a watering can, before we come back to a tool after designing a remote control. So, we still have a lot to do! Moving on.

9 Project 8: Watering can

Now let's move on to the next design project. We would like to create a designer watering can. If we mentally break down the finished watering can into its individual parts, we can see that we need an oval and hollow base body with a recess in the upper area as well as a neck in the front area and a handle, which we will then add to the base body later. It is always very helpful to imagine individual basic bodies and think about how to build them. For the oval base body we want to extrude, we create a 2D sketch on the x-y plane. We then select the "Ellipse" command to draw the oval outline.

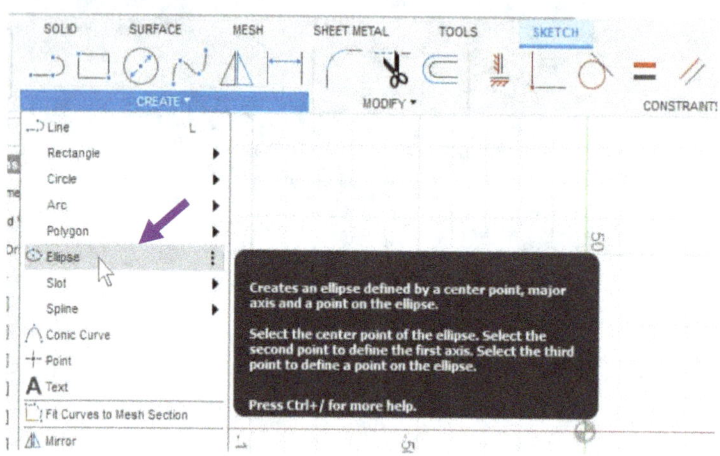

We start at the center point and dimension the width of the ellipse as 140 mm, and the height as 85 mm.

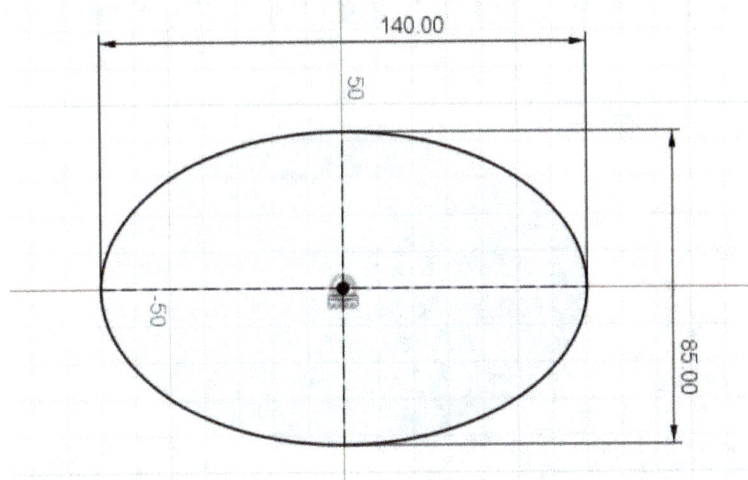

Now we can already finish the 2D sketch. We will now use the "Extrusion" function to create the base body. The watering can is to be 160 mm high.

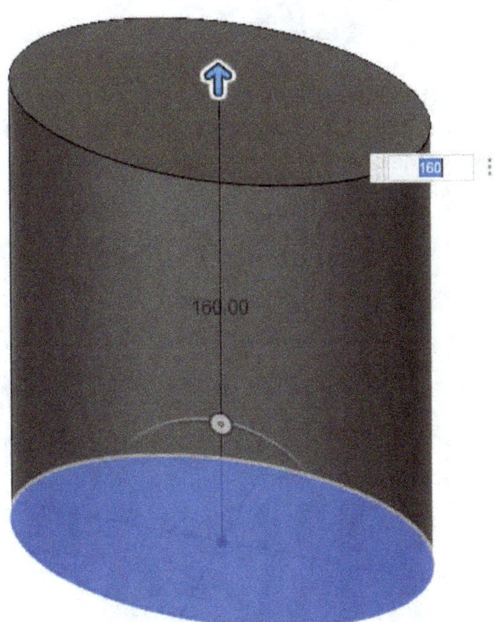

To be able to attach the front neck of the watering can, we first create a parallel plane to the y-z plane with a distance of 65 mm in the next step. This is because the neck must start slightly inside the watering can to ensure a correct transition, as we will see later.

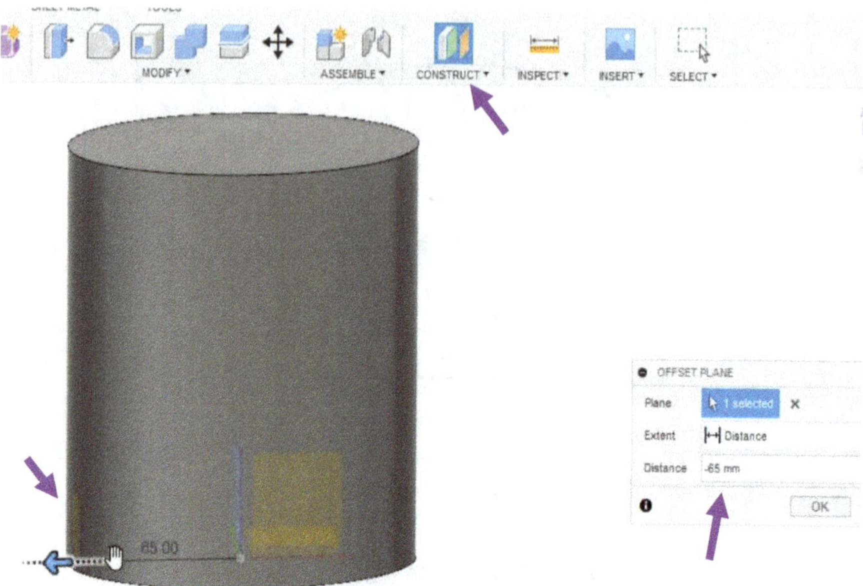

On this plane, we then sketch an ellipse again as the basic profile for the neck of the watering can. This ellipse should sit 20 mm above the bottom of the watering can and be given a vertical link to the origin. The dimensions of the ellipse should be as follows: 10 mm wide and 20 mm high.

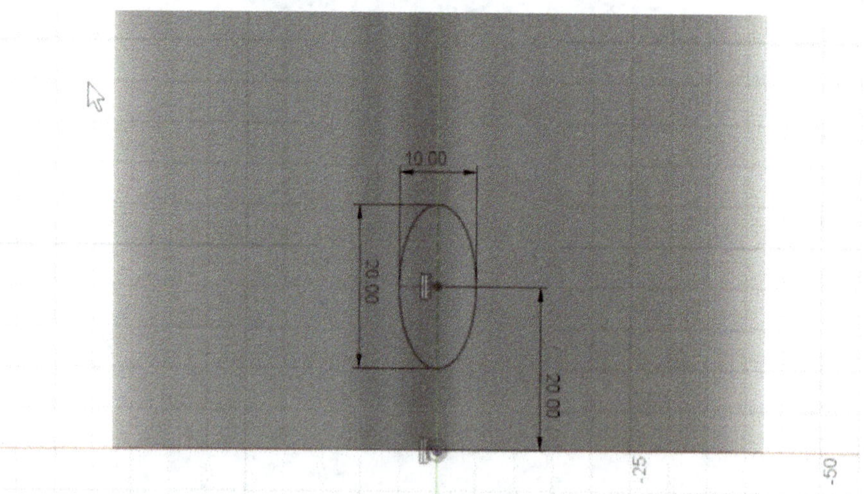

Then we can finish the sketch. We want to create the watering can neck using the "Sweep" function. As you may remember from the beginner's course, we always need a profile and a path for this function. Before we draw this path, we add the front boundary of the watering can neck. To do this, we create a -180 mm "offset" plane to the y-z plane and draw another ellipse on it in the upper area.

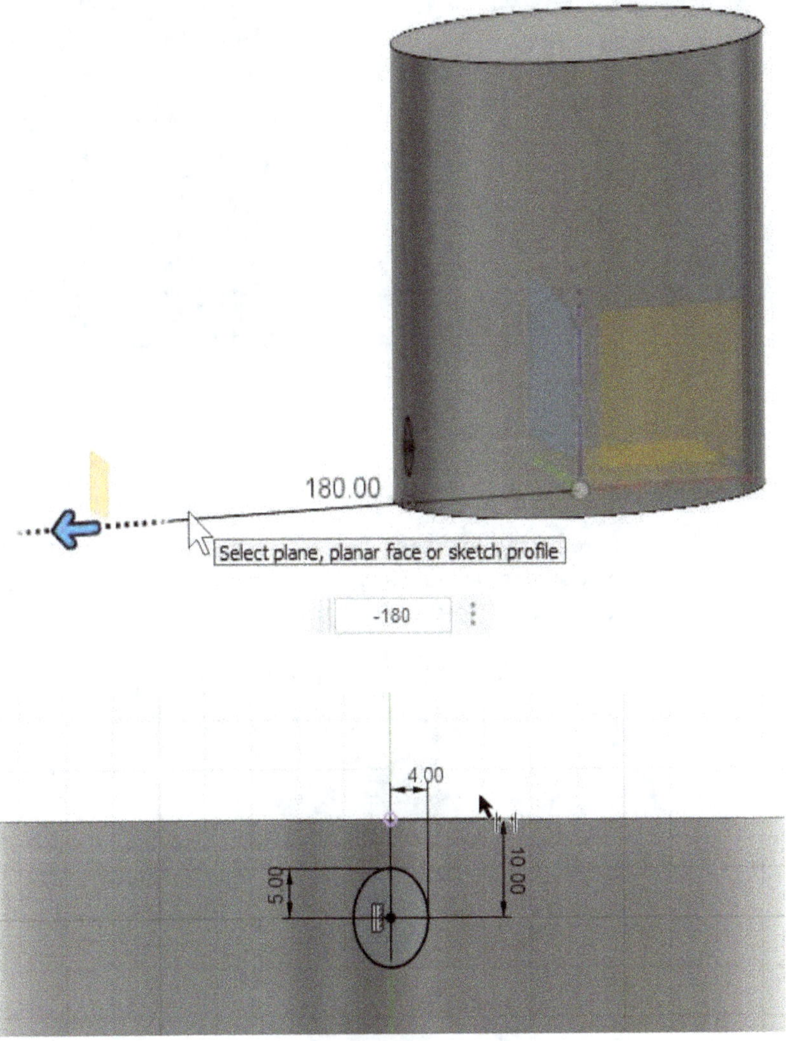

We could also just draw a point, since we only need this sketch for the end position of the path, as we will see in a moment. So, we draw an ellipse with arbitrary dimensions and link it vertically to the origin. The vertical distance to the top of the watering can should be 10 mm. After we finish the sketch, we can start a new sketch on the x-z plane, in which we draw the path for the "Sweep" command. We now simply draw a connection between the two previous sketches for the path, in the form of a 3-point arc, so that we also meet the design requirements. The start and end points must lie on the centers of the two previous sketched ellipses, you may still need to create coincident links for this. The radius of the arc should be 245 mm, for example.

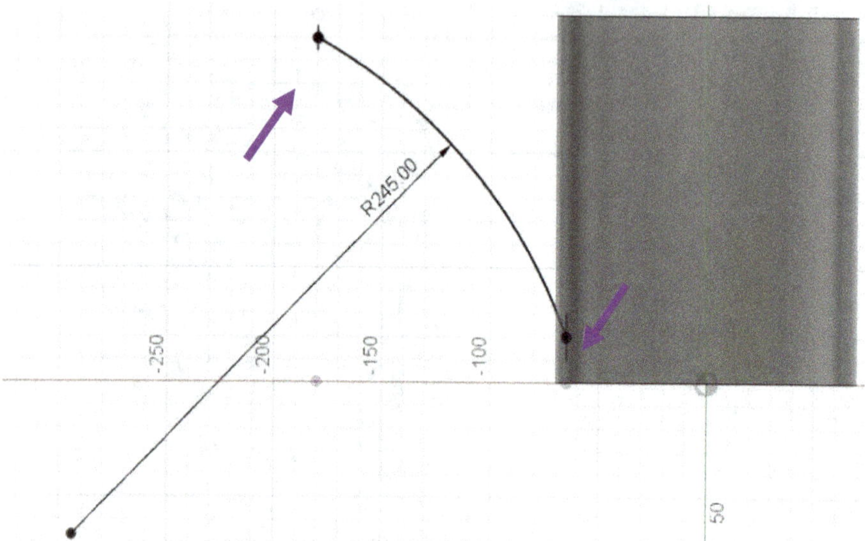

Then we can exit the sketch and select the "Sweep" command. We must then first select the profile of the watering can neck and in the second step, after changing the selection to "Path" in the settings, select the path that corresponds to our arc.

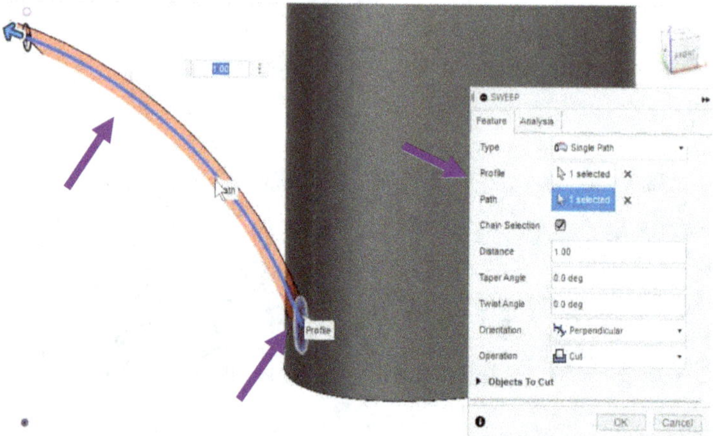

To rotate the spout 180 degrees at the front end, we can then set a twist of 180 degrees in the "Twist Angle" settings. Finally, we need to change the "Operation" to "Join" so that material is generated.

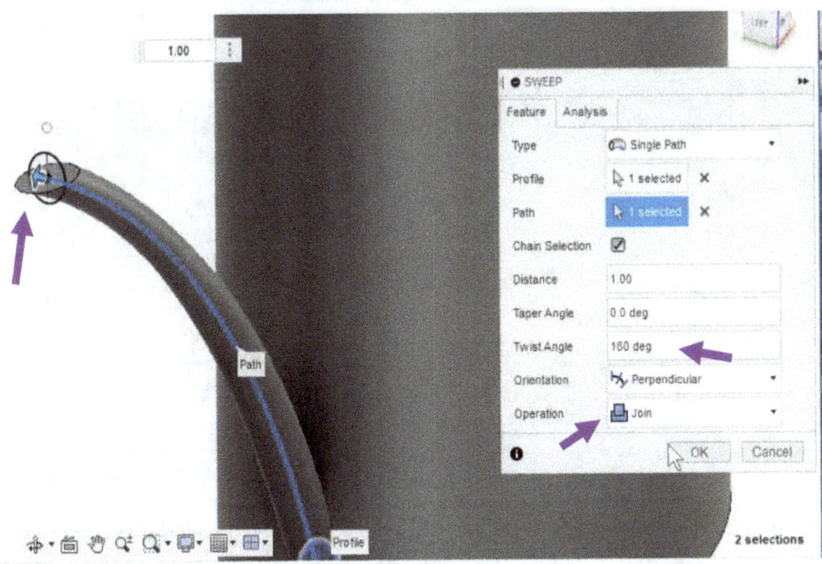

In the next step, we create the oval depression on the top surface of the watering can, which will later be the filling opening. To do this, we draw an ellipse with the following dimensions and as shown on the top surface.

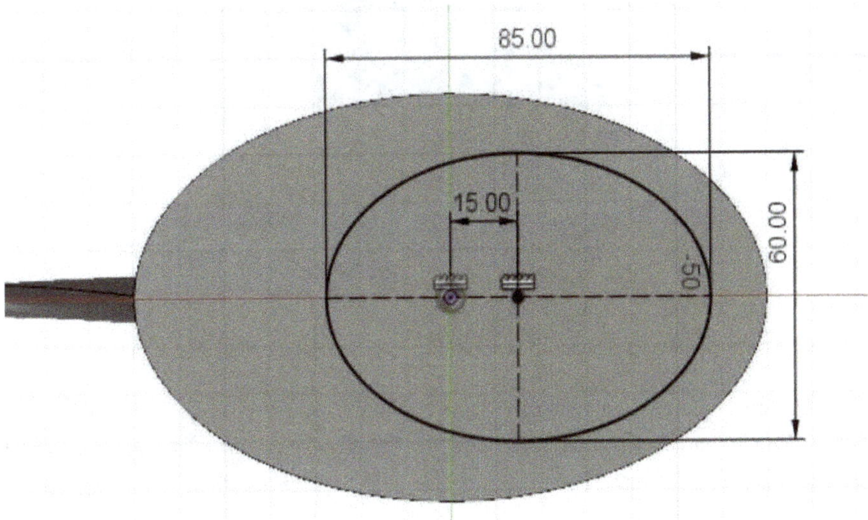

We then extrude this profile -3 mm into the inside of the watering can.

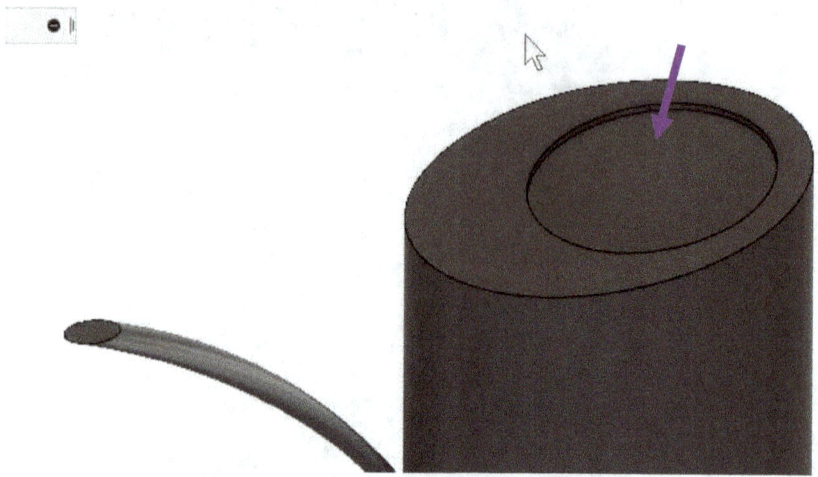

Subsequently, we want to hollow out the base body. How do we do that? Exactly, with the "Shell" command! Select the command, select the surface of the filling area, additionally also select the upper surface of the pouring can neck and define a wall thickness of e.g., 1.5 mm.

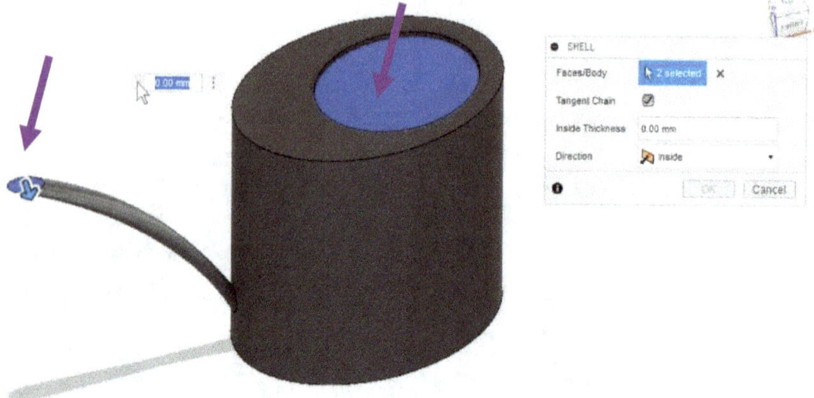

Now we are relatively far, only the handle is missing. We create the handle relatively similar to the watering can neck. So, again with the "Sweep" function. As profile, we draw an ellipse in the back area on an "offset" plane, which should have a distance of 68 mm to the y-z plane.

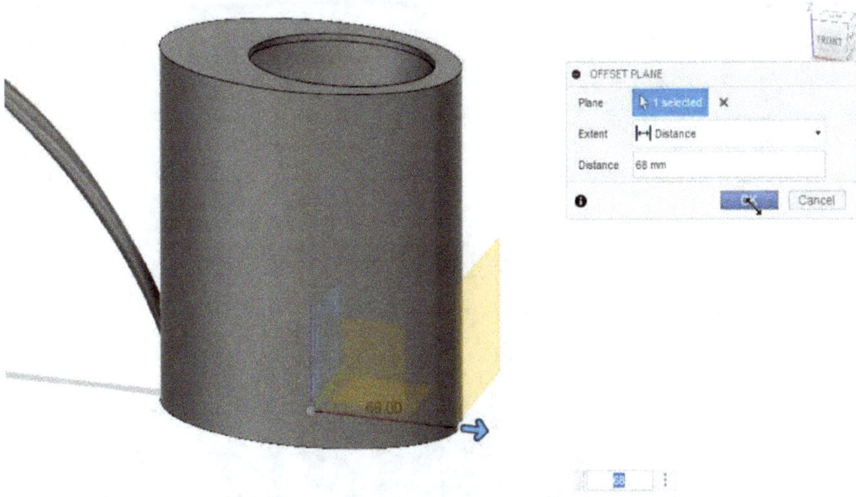

The ellipse should then be 15 mm wide and 7 mm high, as well as have a vertical distance to the origin of 15 mm and sit linked in the center.

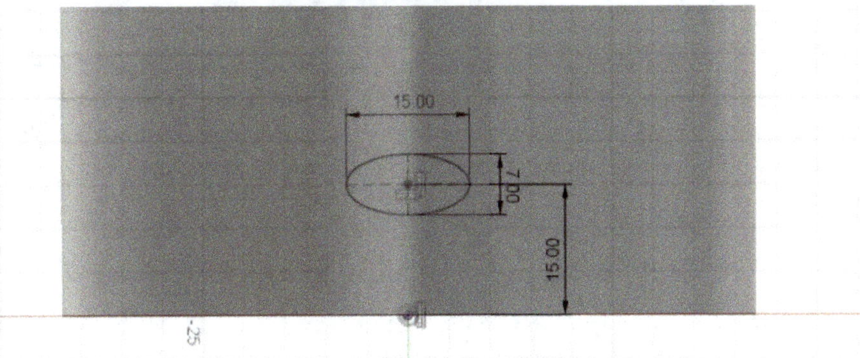

We finish the sketch and then created the path by starting a sketch on the x-z plane. As to the design, the handle of the watering can should be relatively flared and curved. We'll start first with a simple slanted line that needs to start at the center of the ellipse we drew earlier. You may have to create a coincident link. For the handle, we'll draw relatively freely, so we'll save most of the dimensions for now and then define the profile in a different way later. We then add a 3-point arc between the endpoint of the sloped line and the centerline. At the bottom, the arc should sit tangent to the line, but otherwise you are free to shape it however you like.

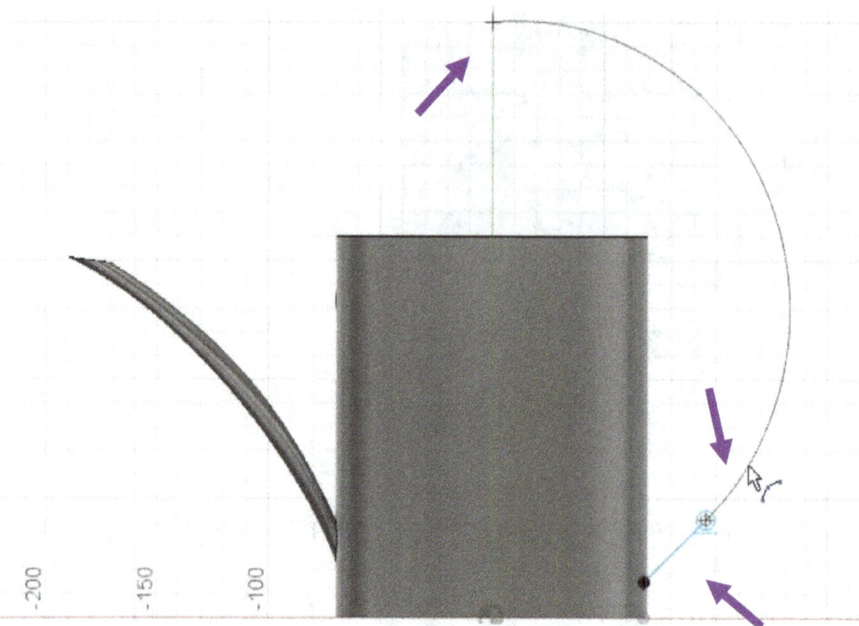

Then we add another oblique line in the front upper part of the watering can. This must start inside so that the edges of the handle are modeled correctly afterwards. We dimensioned a 4 mm distance from the front top corner point for this. We will complete the path with two more 3-point arcs, which we will also set tangential to each other again.

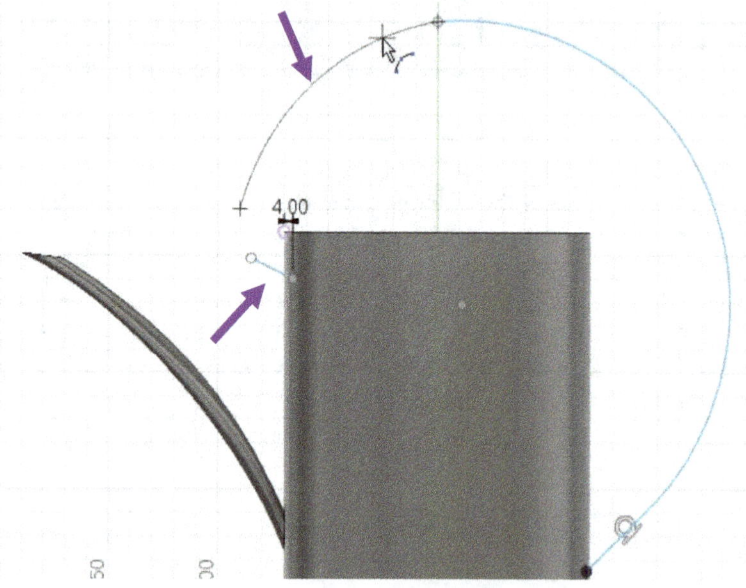

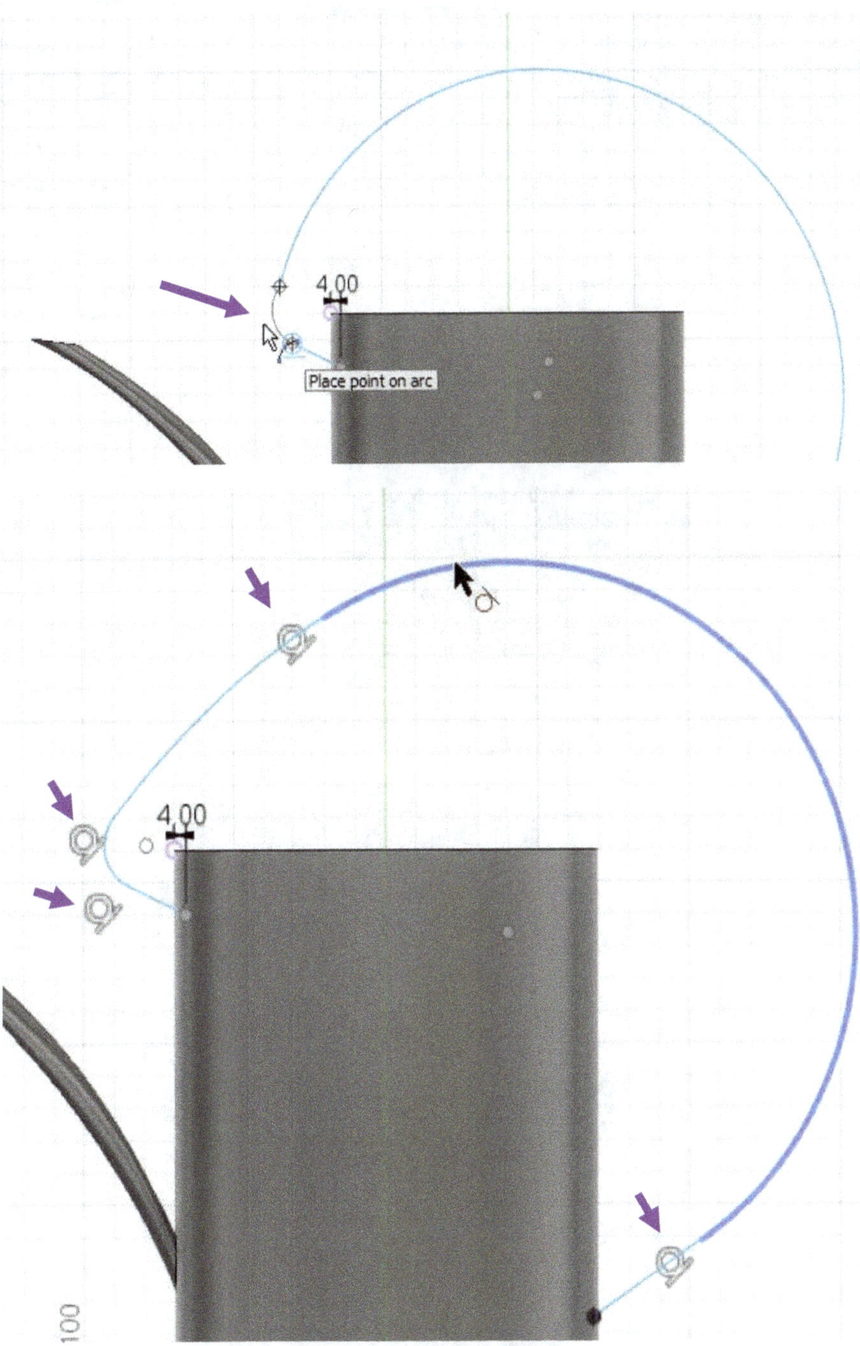

We now simply save the relatively complex dimensioning for the complete definition of the profile. Since we basically have no dimension specifications and have sketched freehand, this is also justifiable. To define the profile in the current position, we use the "Constraint": "Fix". Mark all profile sections including corner points and select the small lock symbol at the "Constraints".

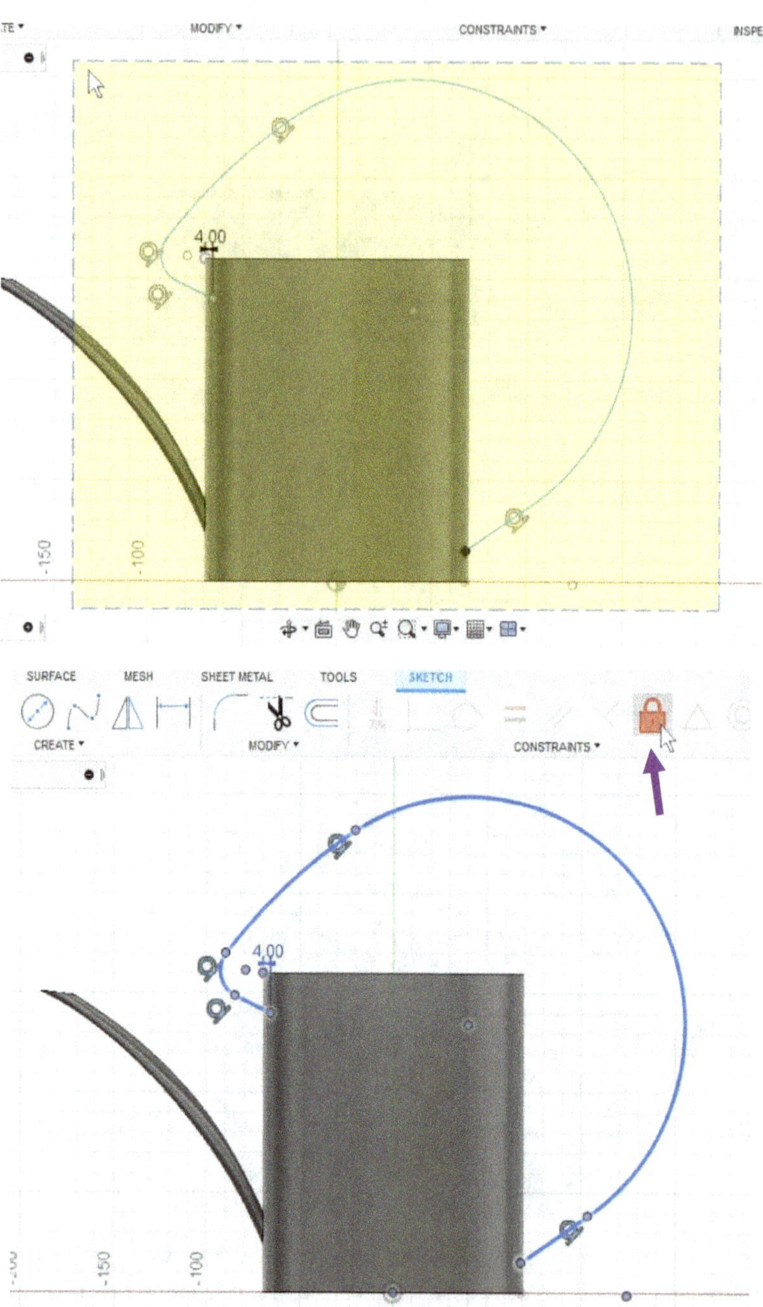

The profile then turns green and is fully fixed in the plane. This is the easy or quick way to fully define a sketch. After we have finished the sketch, we can create the handle with the "Sweep" command. To do this, select the profile and the path as before.

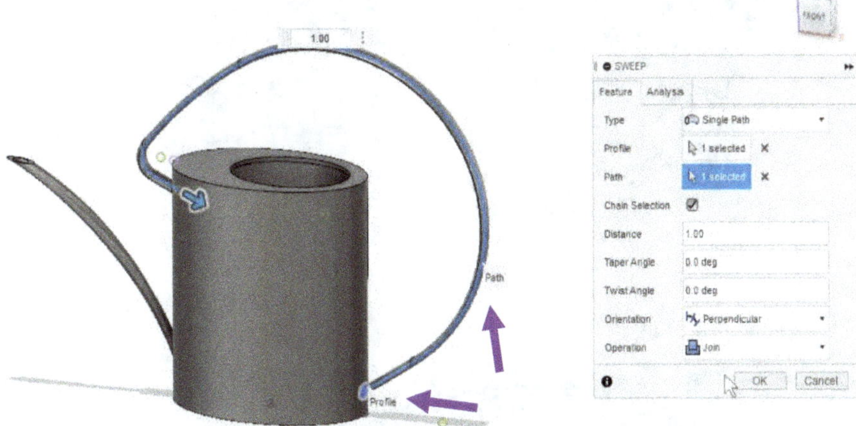

In the penultimate step, we create a few fillets as follows: 5 mm for the lower edge, also 5 mm for the two upper edges, 2 mm for the edges of the sprue parts and 0.5 mm for the pouring can spout.

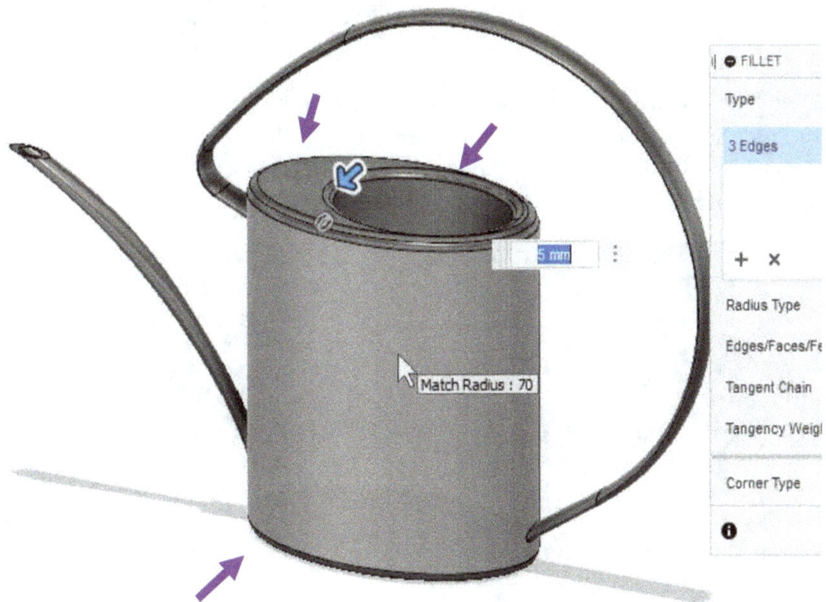

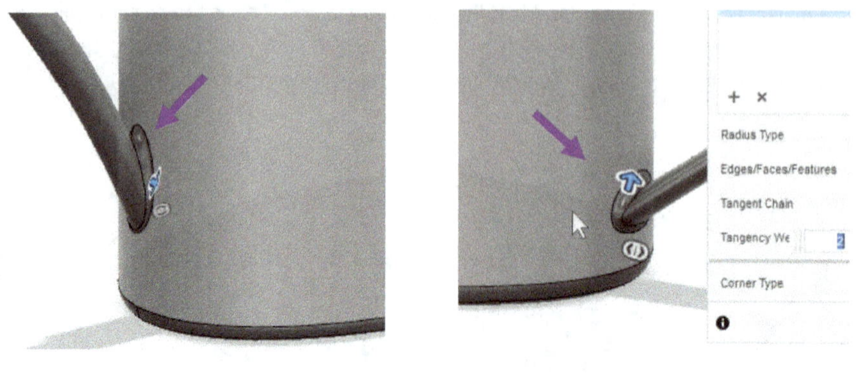

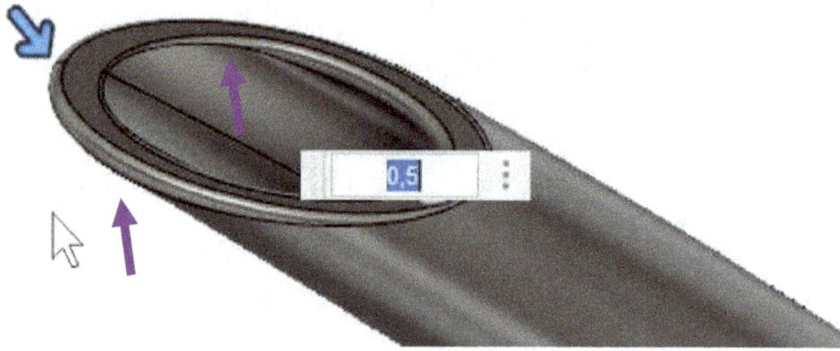

If we then take a look inside the watering can, we notice that remnants of the handle protrude into the interior, these are necessary so that the "Sweep" command can properly model the handle on the outer curves. We can now delete these remnants simply by right-clicking and selecting "Delete".

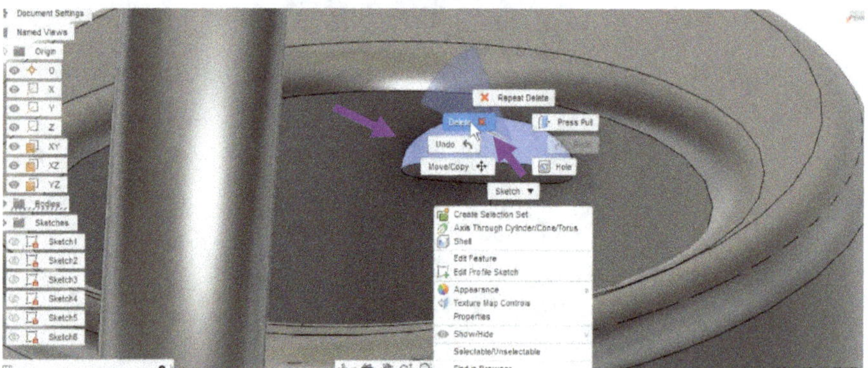

Excellent! As a final step, we would like to change the appearance a bit. For example, we could choose the appearance of a green glossy plastic surface.

The watering can is done. With a 3D printer, you could now print it out. Use my 3D printing beginner course if you are interested in this topic!

In the next chapter, we will create a mockup of a remote control.

10 Project 9: Remote control

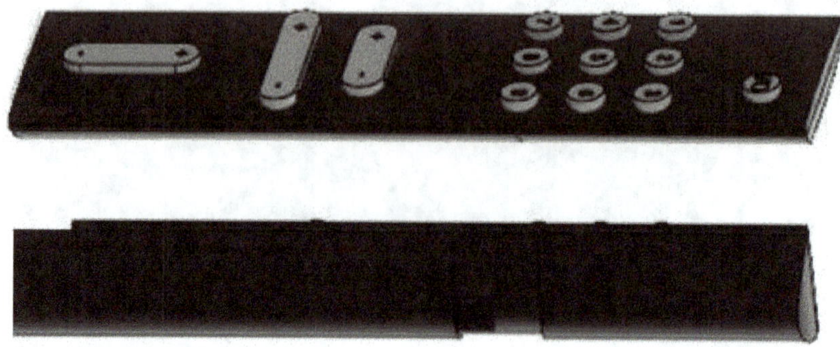

In this chapter, we want to create a remote control that will have a battery compartment with a slide-on cover, as well as some buttons. Normally, such a remote control is not createed in one piece, but from several injection molded parts. In this case, however, we will create only one mockup, which we will make from one piece. For the basic body, which has an oval shape and which we will create by extrusion, we first need a 2D sketch on the x-y plane. We start for the shape of the cross-section with two 2 mm long vertical lines, one of which we place to the left and one to the right of the origin. The distance between these two lines should be 40 mm. The distance to the origin should be 20 mm so that the lines sit symmetrically to the centerline. We also create a horizontal link between the line start point and the origin. Next is a 3-point arc that connects the lower part and should have a radius of 25 mm.

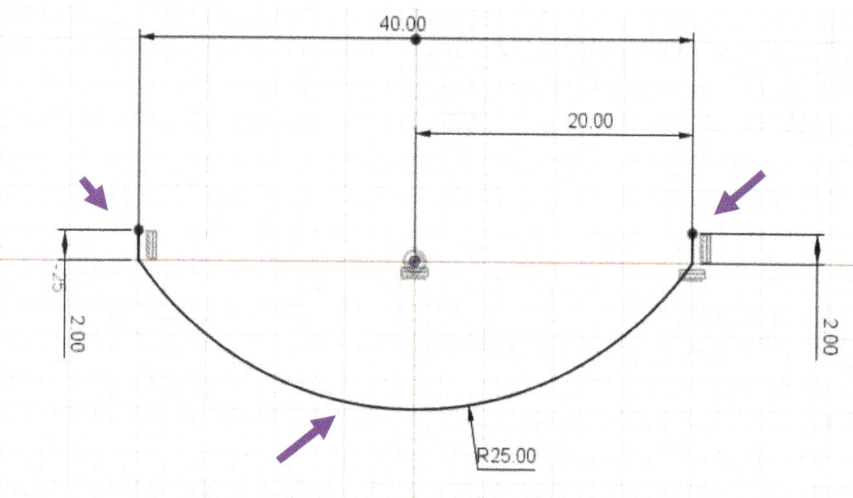

We place another sheet with a 200 mm radius on the upper side. Finally, we round the four remaining edges with 1 mm each.

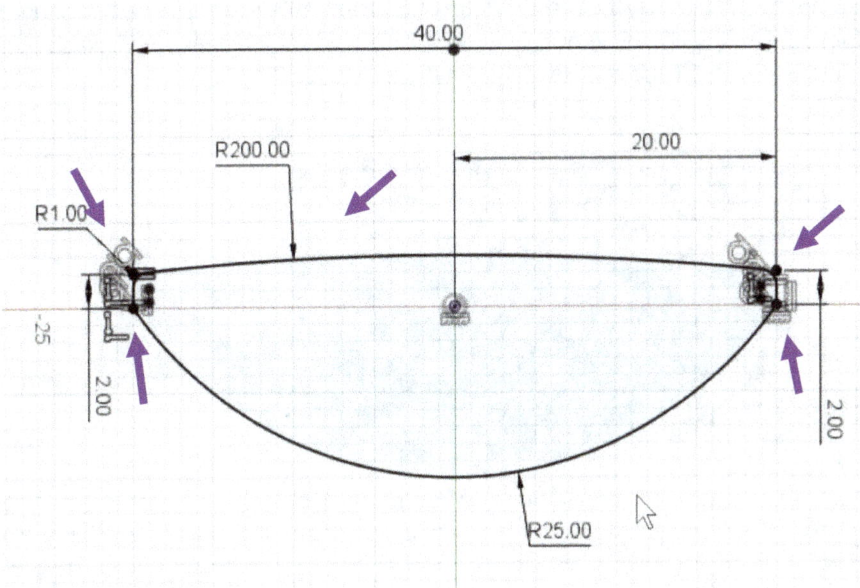

Then follows a symmetrical extrusion with 75 mm spacing, so that our basic body takes shape.

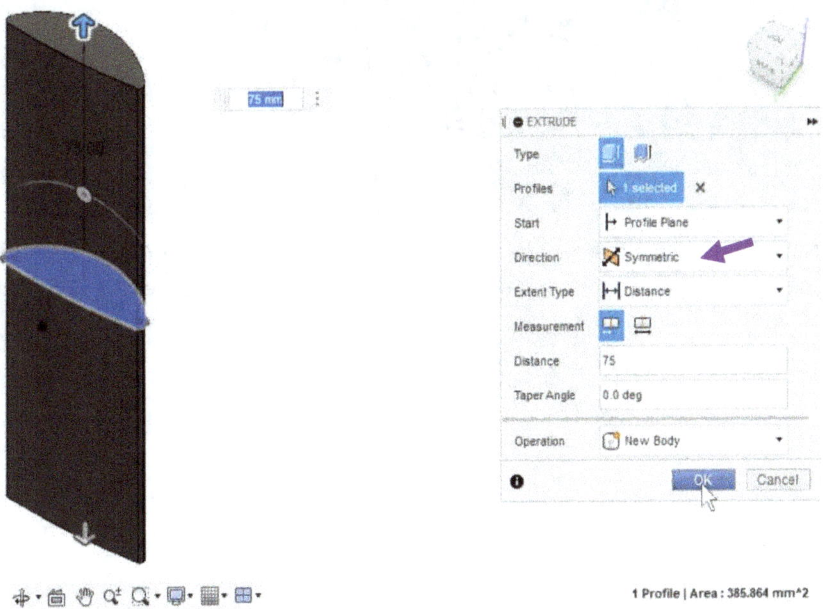

We want to bevel the upper surface of the remote control a little. We do this with a profile on the side surface, which we then use to remove material from the base body. Furthermore, we draw the profile on the y-z plane in the upper part of the remote control. The initial geometry is a horizontal line whose start and end points are coincident with the upper edge of the remote control, as shown.

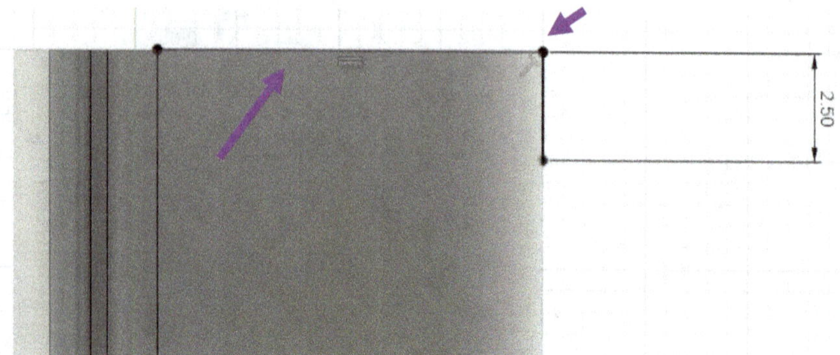

Then we sketch a 2.5 mm vertical line down the right edge and connect the two remaining end points of the geometry with a 3-point arc. This is given a radius of 40 mm.

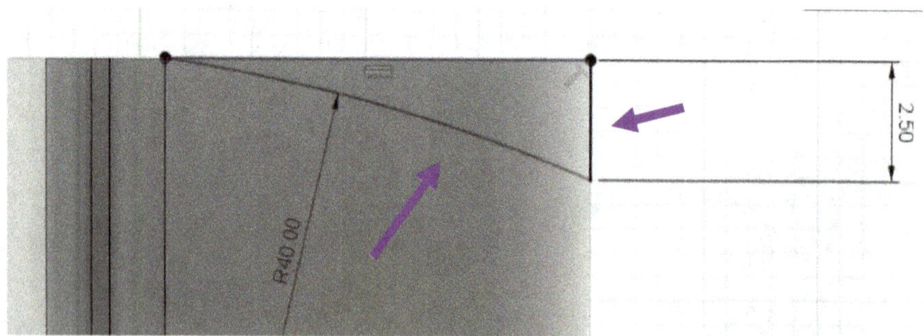

Now that we have sketched on the center plane, we need to extrude the profile from the center, e.g., -20 mm with the "Symmetric" and "Cut" option. Now we have a coherent, flattened deck side.

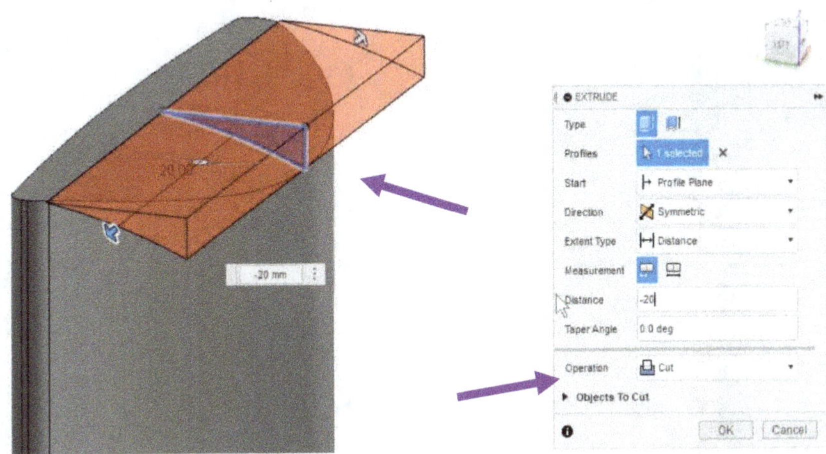

Next, we create a 20 mm "offset" plane to create a sketch for the battery cover cutout.

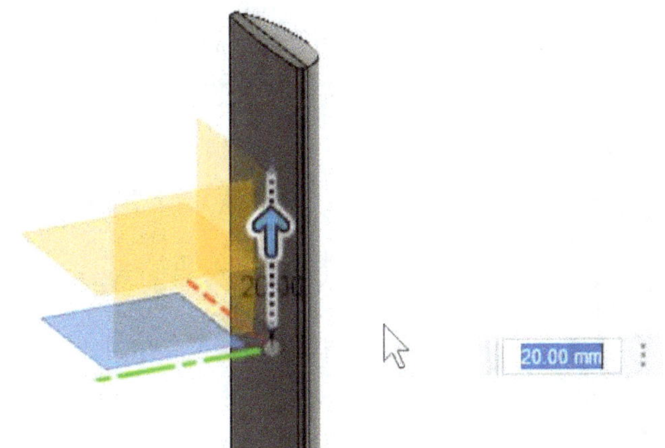

At this plane, we outline the following profile:

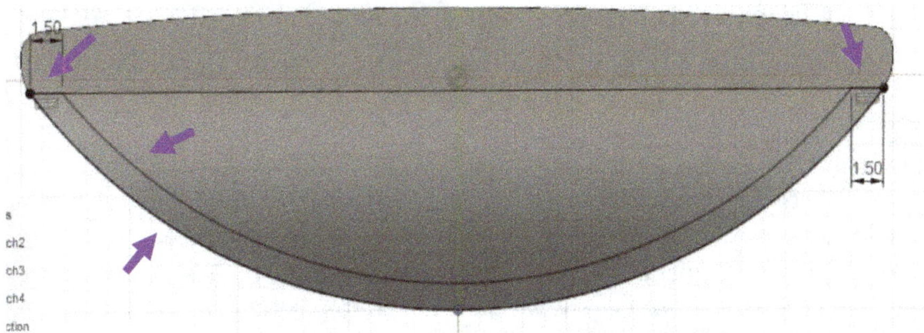

We then cut away this profile in 3D mode with the help of an extrusion, first downwards -95 mm.

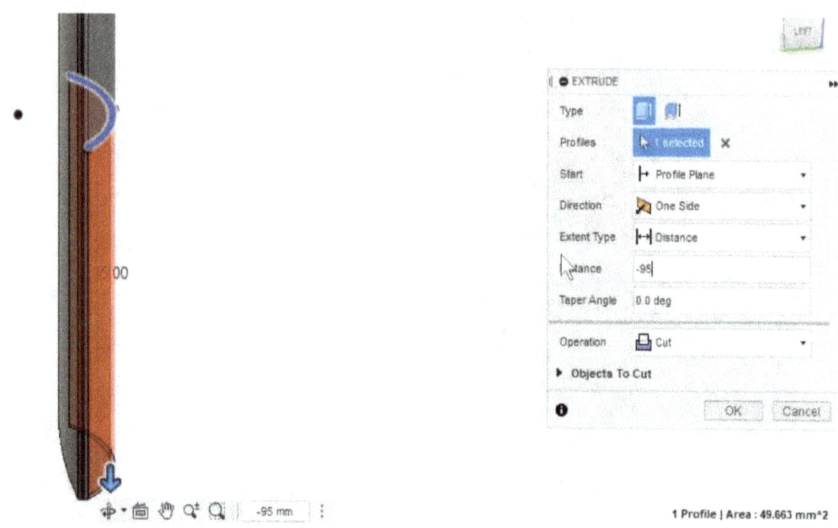

In the next step, we then use the same profile again to create an exact-fit new body or component for the lid from it. First, let's select: Body.

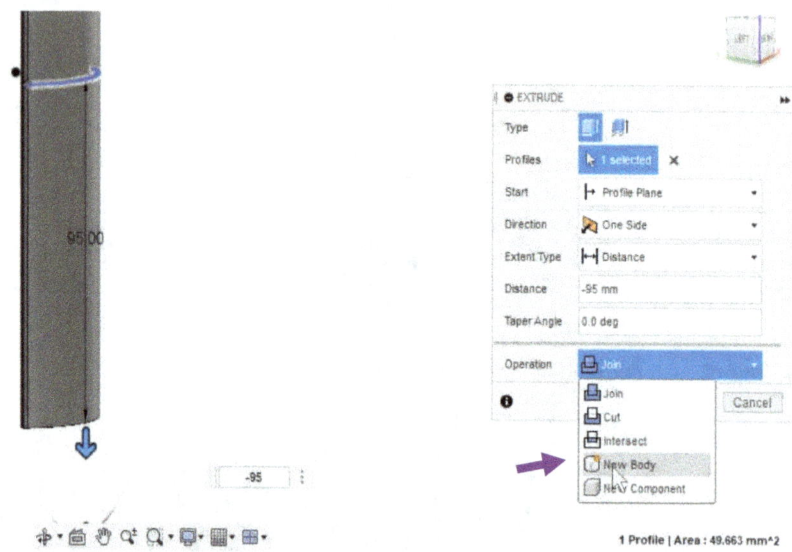

As we can now see, we now have two separate bodies, but since these are bodies, we cannot move them away from each other. So, we can't create a joint here either. But since these are two separate parts, we want to create a joint. So, we would have better set "component". But, don't worry, we didn't do this step for nothing, we will now use the "New Component" command and check "From Bodies" to create a new component from the body.

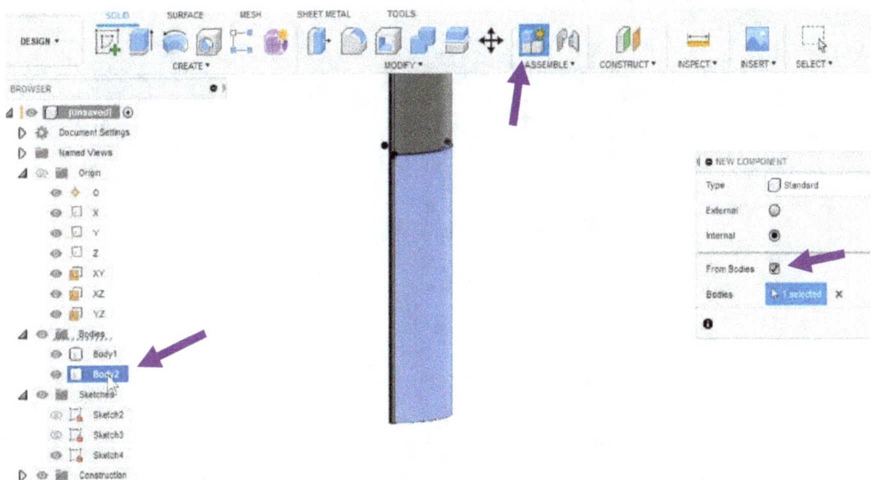

In the part browser, we then see that the second body is no longer present, but a component has been added instead. Now we can connect the two components with a joint. To do this, we select, for example, the following joint origins and the joint type "Slider".

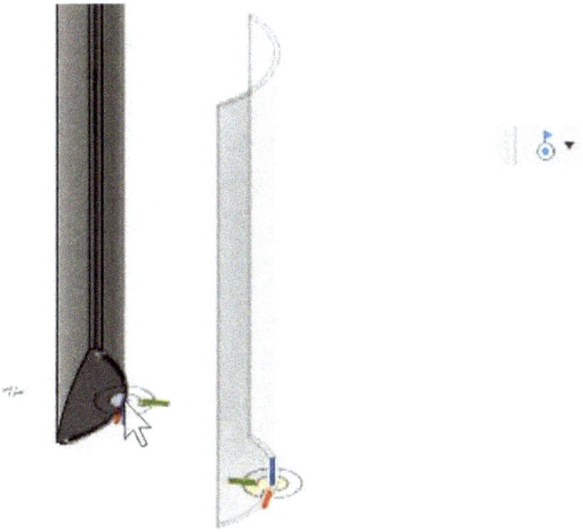

For the upper stop point, we then still need to set the end point by right-clicking on the joint in the timeline or in the part browser and selecting "Edit Joint Limits".

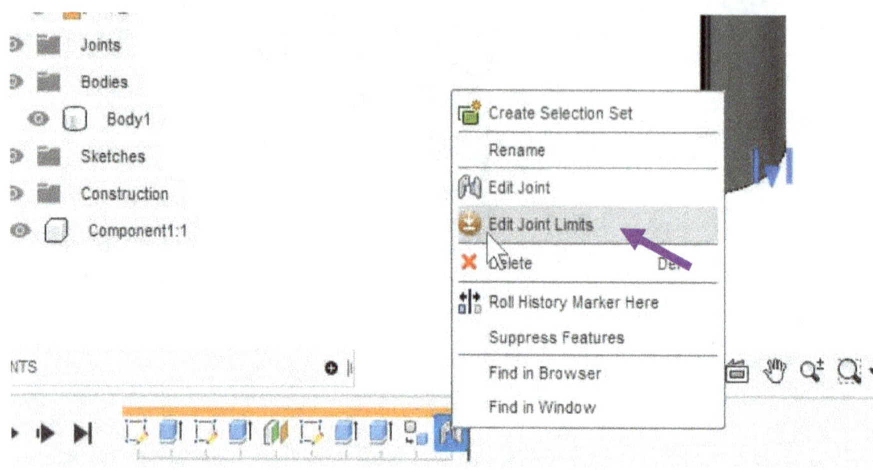

This works by activating the "Minimum" option. The set value of 0 mm already fits because we have linked the lid for the battery compartment in the closed state.

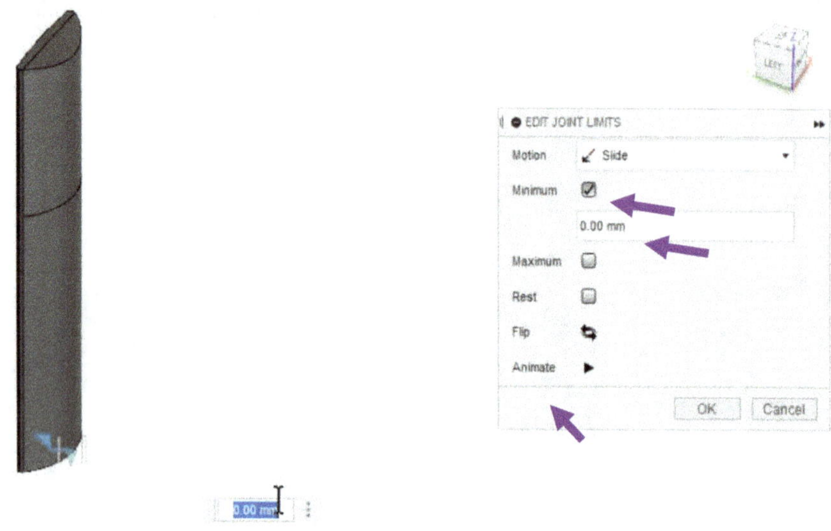

We can convince ourselves of the correctness by clicking on "Animate" in the settings. Now we can only move the battery cover to the upper stop point.

Next, we create a cutout to represent the battery compartment. To achieve this, we create a parallel plane to the x-z plane with a distance of -2.5 mm. On this plane, we draw the following rectangular profile:

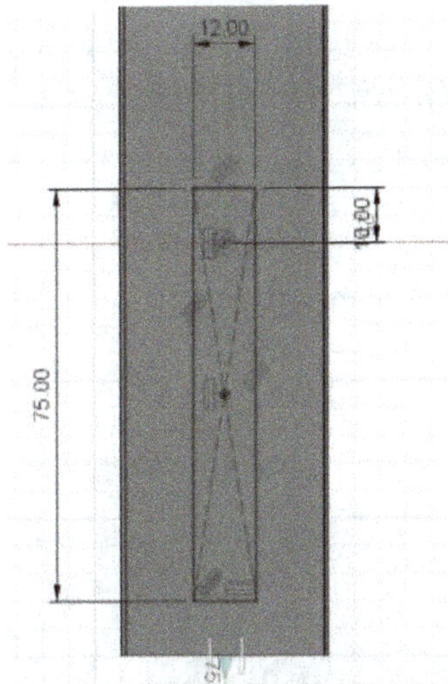

Before we extrude the rectangular profile, we must first slide on the lid so that it is not accidentally cut out as well. We then cut -10 mm with the "Extrusion" command and get the battery compartment this way.

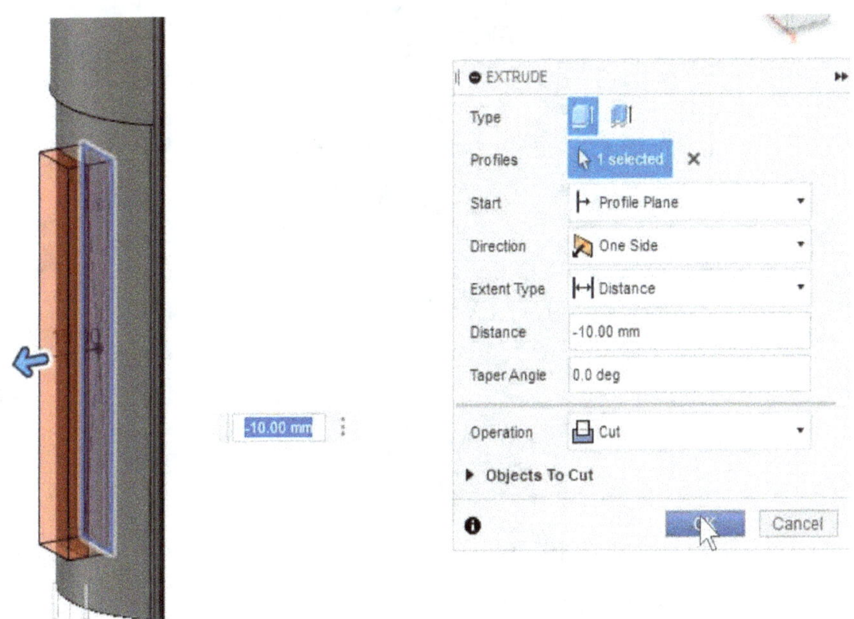

So that the front side doesn't remain as blank as it still is, we now get to work on the sketches for the keys of the remote control. For this, we sketch on the x-z plane. So, we extrude from the inside. We have to do this because the front surface of the remote is curved. If we were to sketch on this curved surface, the side transitions of the buttons would not be linked to the surface. For practice purposes, why don't you try this out, and you'll understand what I mean in a moment.

So, as we said, we sketch on the x-z plane. For the first key, the on/off-key, we sketch a circle with a diameter of 7 mm in the upper-right corner and position the circle with 9 mm or 65 mm to the origin. The next key also gets a 7 mm circle, which should be positioned with 12.5 mm or 45 mm to the origin.

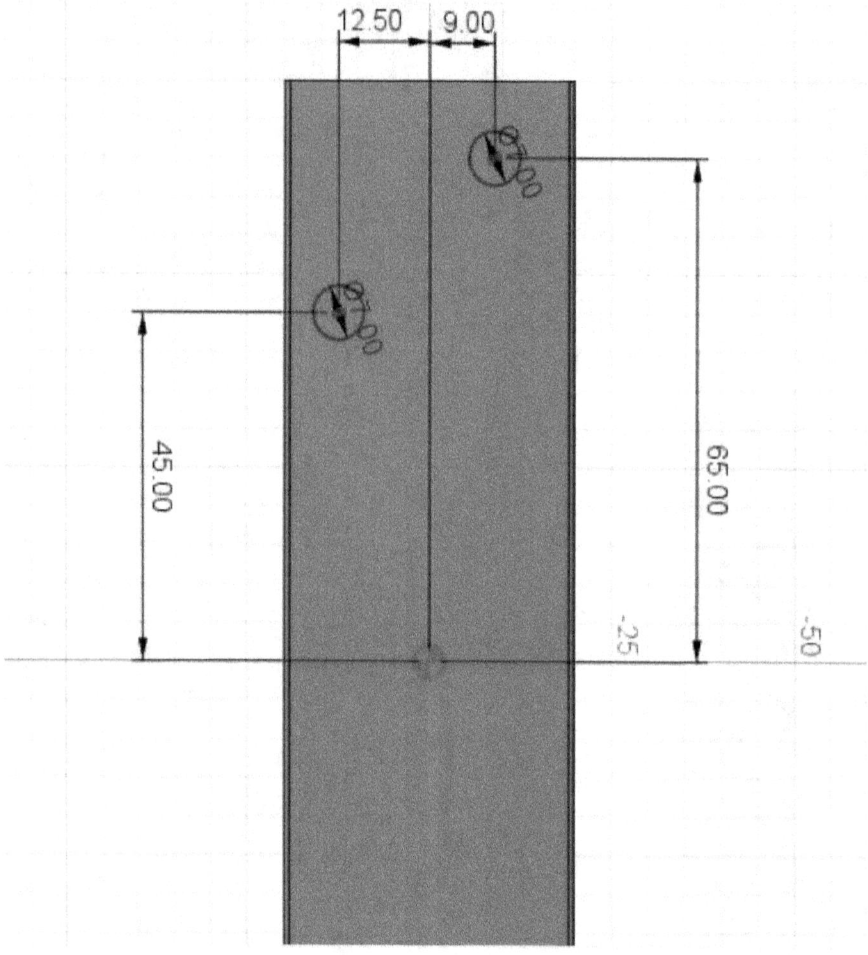

Using the "Rectangular Pattern" command from the "Create" menu, we now create a keypad. To do this, select the circle and drag the displayed arrows to the right and downwards. We want three circles each in x-direction and in z-direction, the number is already set here. We then set a distance of -25 mm in x-direction and +25 mm in z-direction.

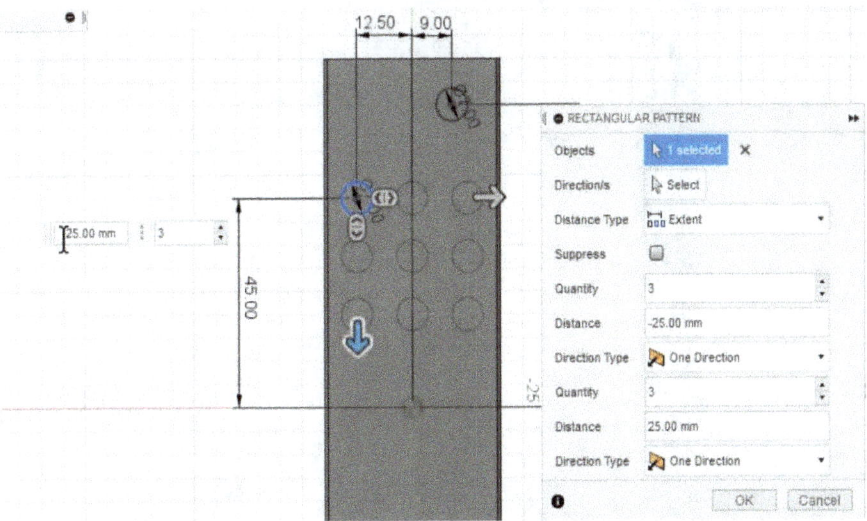

The last three keys should be sketched from oblong holes and two of them should be arranged horizontally, one of them vertically. This should then look like this, including dimensions.

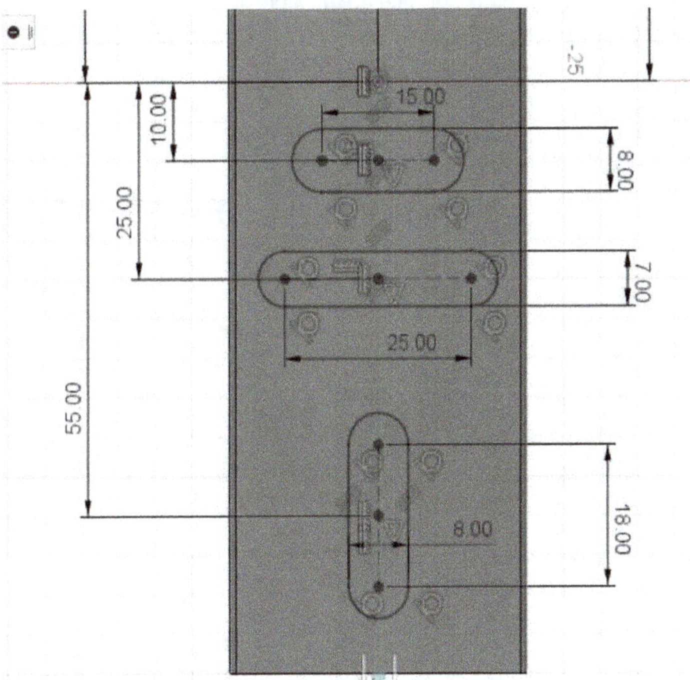

Then we can finish the sketch and extrude the keys 4.5 mm. The "Operation" must then say "New Body".

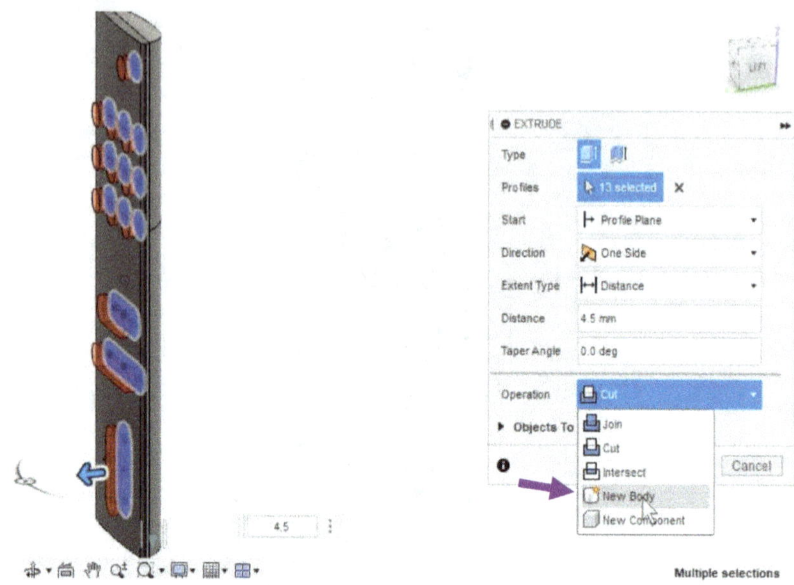

Since we are only drawing a mockup, the keys are connected to the housing and are not functional, but we would still like to be able to differentiate the appearance compared to the base body. We can then cover the base body and also the battery cover with a glossy black color, for example.

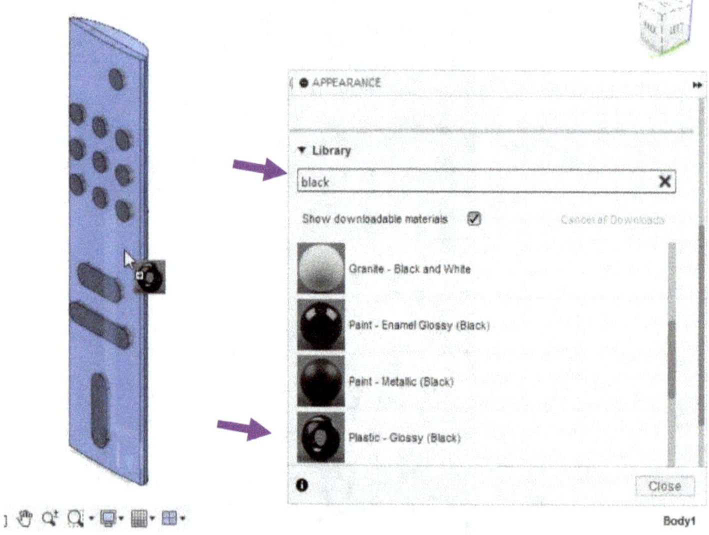

The keys, on the other hand, we cover with a gray glossy color, for example.

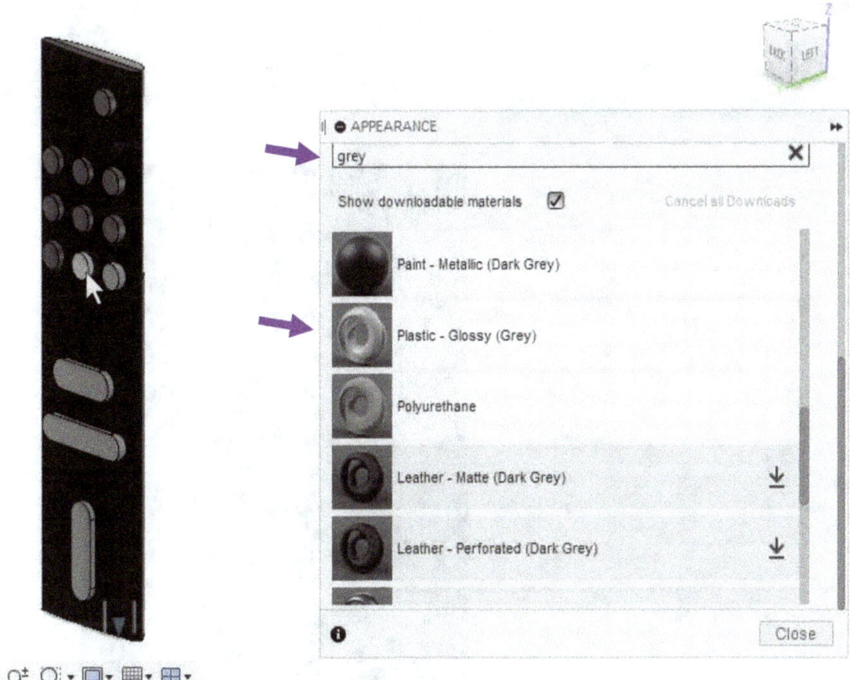

Now we are almost finished. As a last step, we want to label the keys. We do this by embossing the letters and numbers with the "Emboss / Deboss" command. To do this, we first need a sketch of the letters and numbers. First, we create a parallel plane to the x-z plane, which should extend to the surface of the keys. To do this, simply click on the surface and the dimension will be determined automatically.

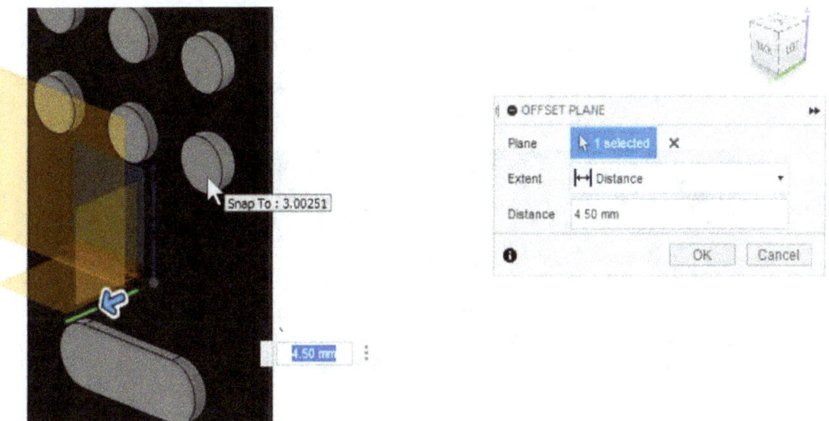

Now, to create letters, numbers, and symbols relatively quickly and very easily, we use the "Text" command from the "Create" menu in the 2D sketch area.

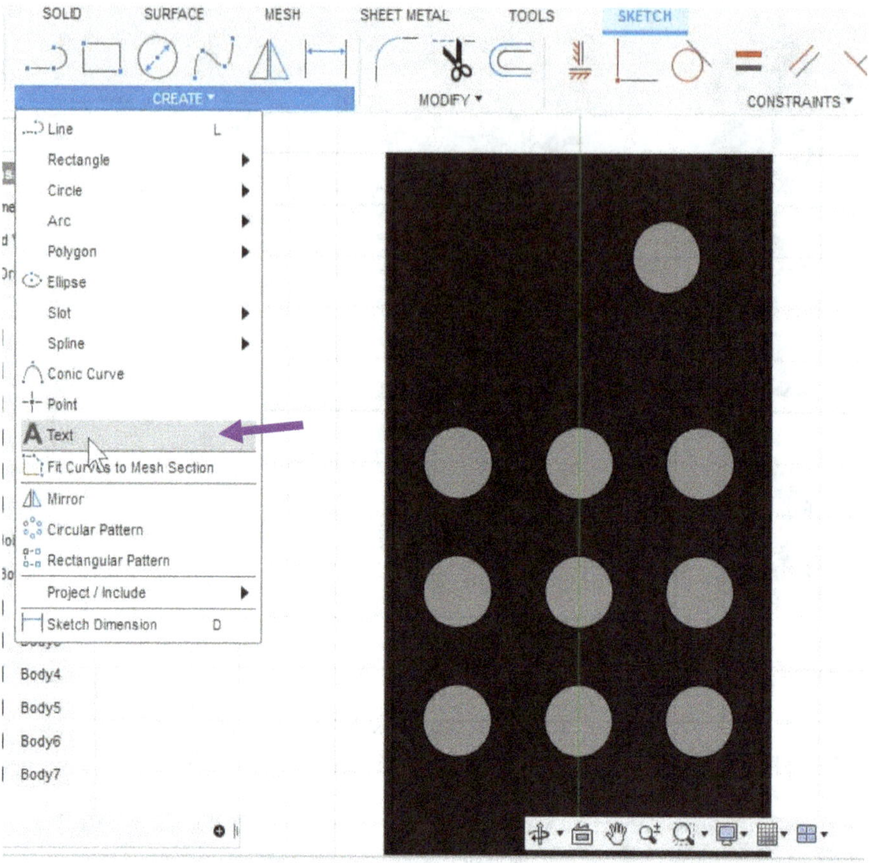

As type, we need a simple text. Then we need to draw a bounding box for the text content. Pretty much like in Microsoft Word or similar programs. We draw the first text box in the area of the first button and enter a text, e.g., "I/O" for the on-off switch. In the settings we can change the text type, the font size and the alignment.

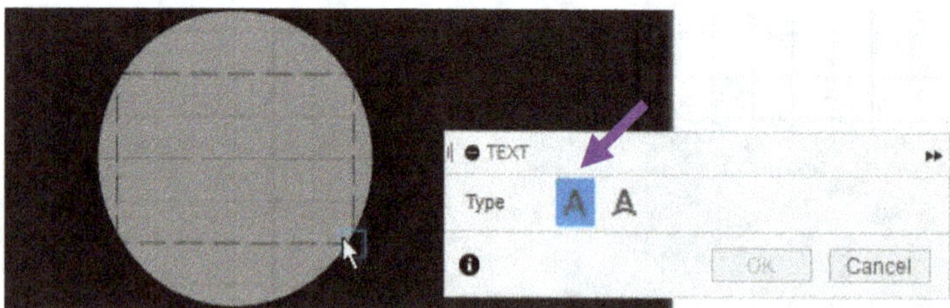

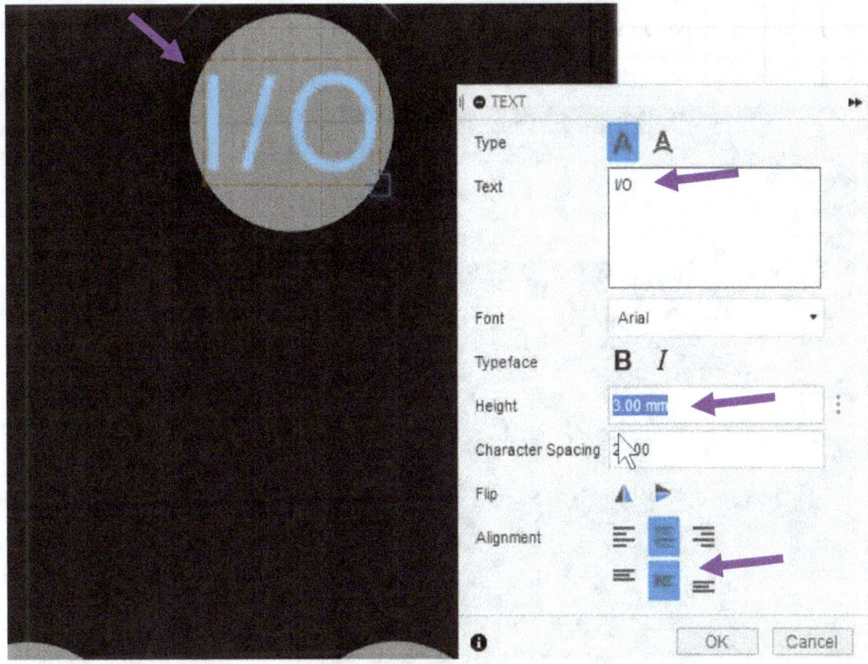

For the second range of keys, we drag a new text box, but this time across all the keys as shown. We then enter the numbers from 1 to 9 and use the settings to position them so that they sit correctly on the keys. For example, we make two paragraphs between each row and set the Character Spacing setting to 270. We also make a space between the numbers. Finally, we define the text height with the value 2.7, so that the numbers sit reasonably accurately and centered on the key fields.

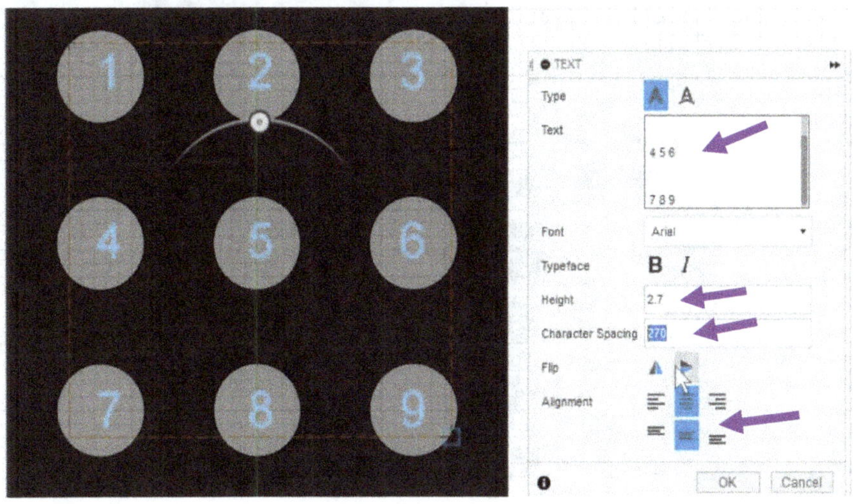

We will do the same with the three lower buttons. Here we want to create a "+" and a "-" symbol each.

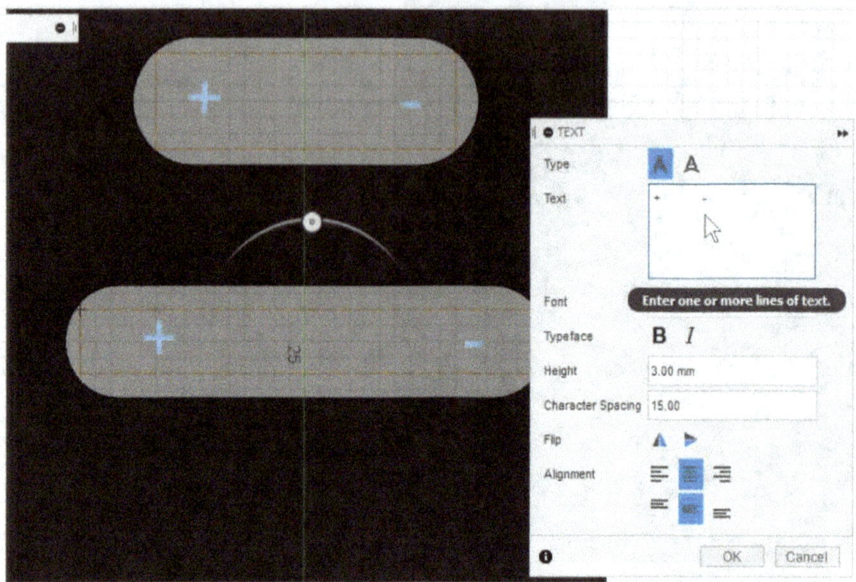

For embossing, we could now best use the "Emboss" command or its "Deboss" option.

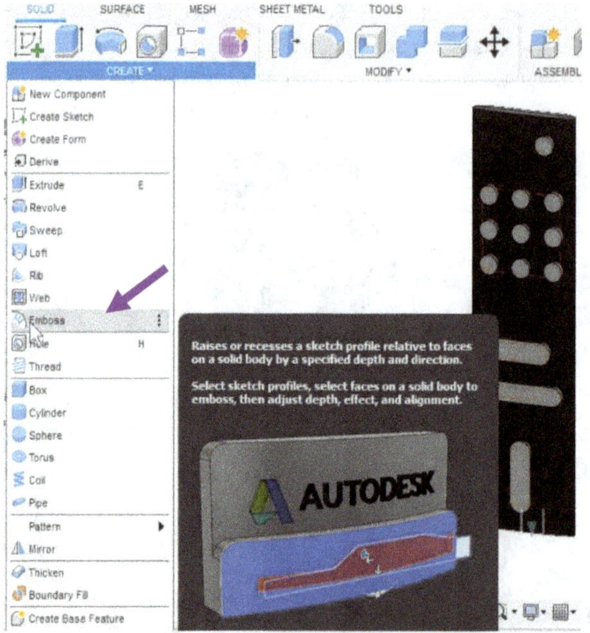

Since we always have to select an embossing surface in addition to a profile with this command, we would have to execute a separate command for each key here. This embossing can be done easier and faster with "Extrude" in this case. We will use the "Emboss / Deboss" command again for illustration in the last project. For the extrusion, we now simply select all text fields and extrude - 0.2 mm with the "Cut" option.

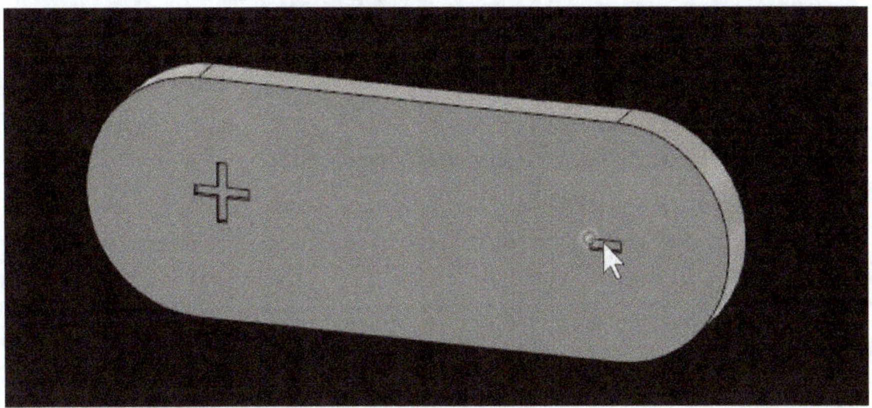

Now we are almost done with this project. Finally, we create a few fillets as usual. For the two lower edges, we choose a radius of 0.5 mm.

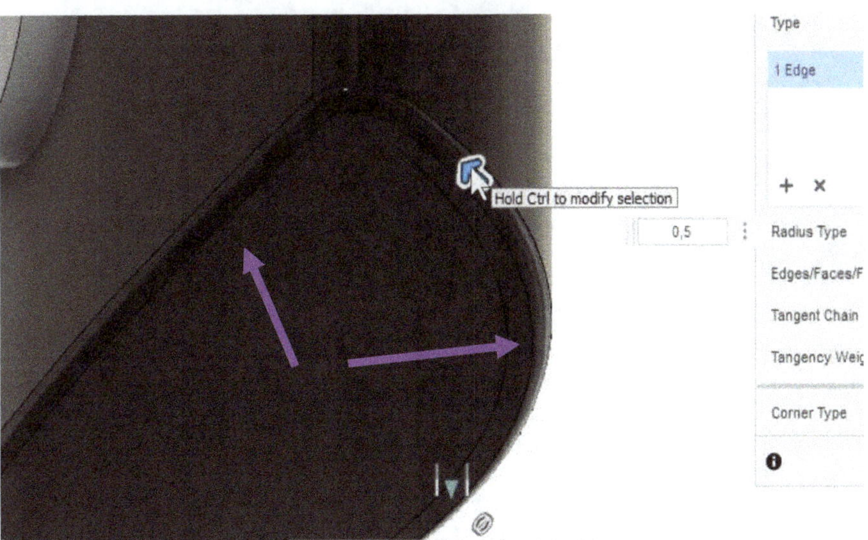

For the edges of the keys we select a fillet radius of 0.1 mm, simply select the cover surfaces.

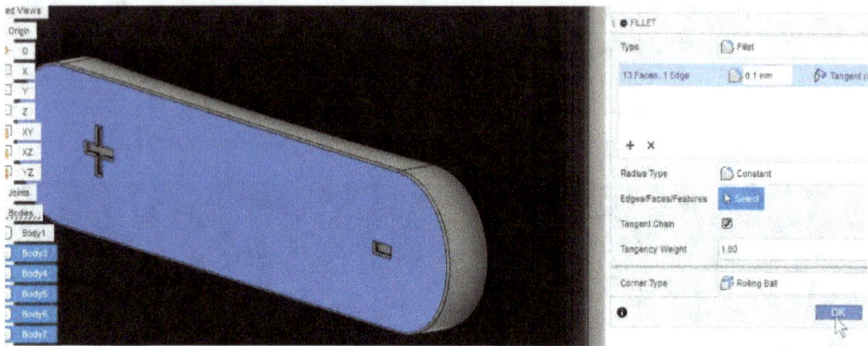

Now we have one remaining design project. In the last project, we will design a water pump wrench or pipe wrench that will be pretty cool. So, it's still worth continuing!

11 Project 10: Water pump pliers

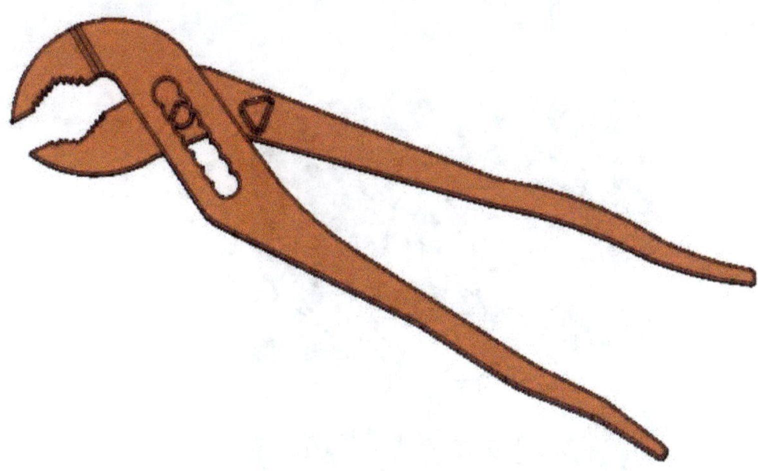

In this chapter, we will create a water pump pliers or pipe wrench, which should look like this:

To create this relatively complex geometry or part, we use a trick. If we have an image of a part, we can simply trace its cross-section in Fusion 360 from that image.

All we have to do is load the image into the program. You can easily find such an image of a component, or in the case of the pliers, using Google Image Search.

It doesn't have to be exactly the same image as here either, but make sure it's taken as vertically as possible from above. To get the image into the program, use the "Canvas" command from the "Insert" menu.

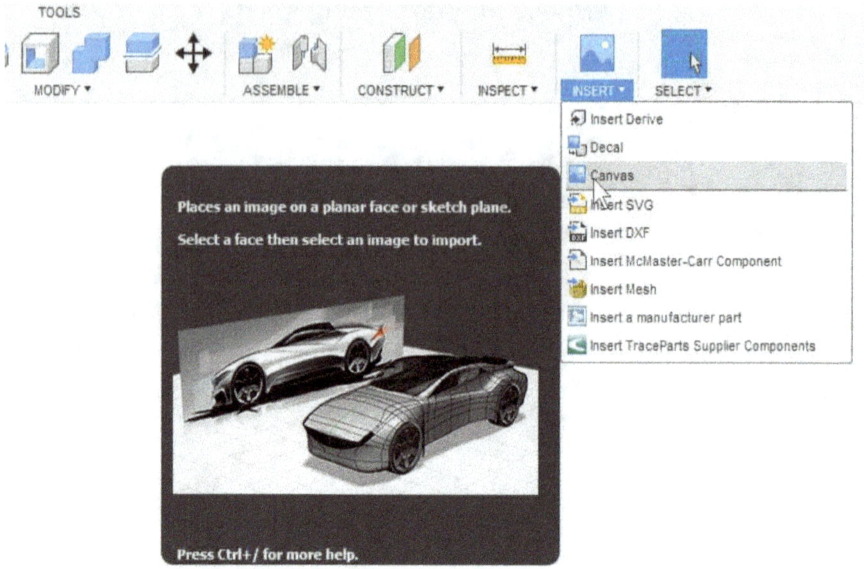

We select "Insert from my computer" and specify the path of the image.

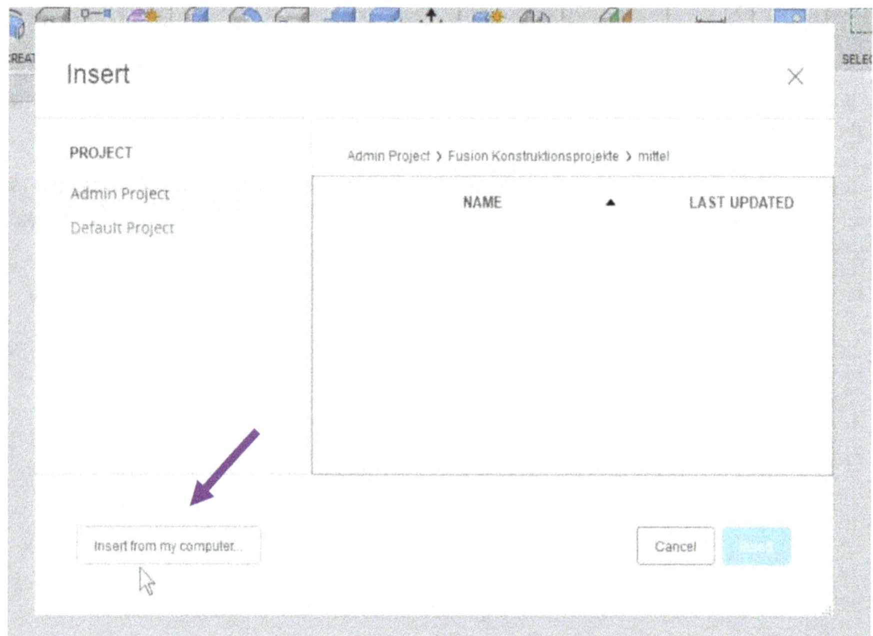

Then we need to select a layer on which to place the image. For example, the x-y plane, since we want to look at the tongs from above. In the settings, we can then move or scale the image. For example, we scale the image in the x-y plane by a factor of 16.

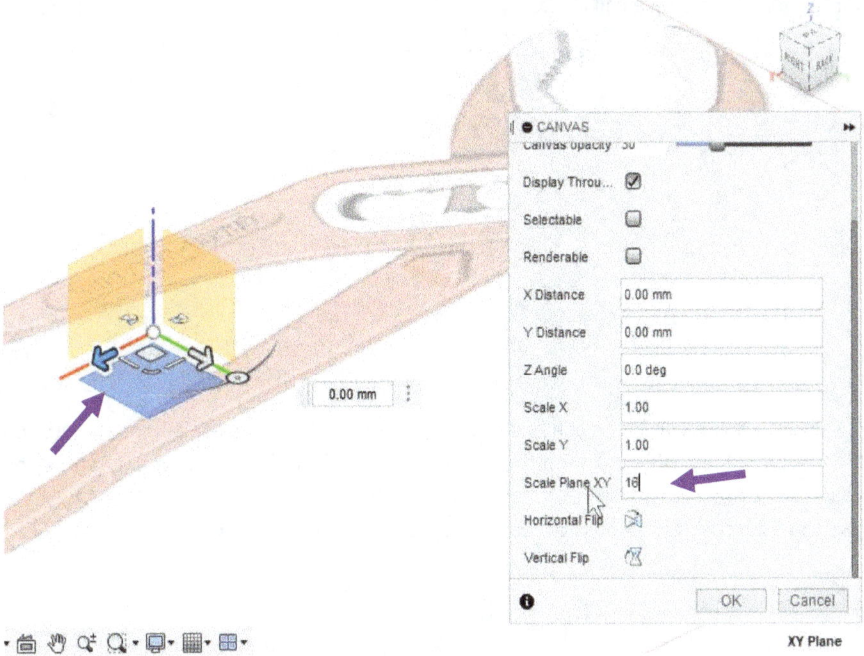

I tried this factor in advance so that the dimensions of the pliers would eventually make sense. Moreover, we can change the transparency of the image in the settings if we want. For example, we set this to 30.

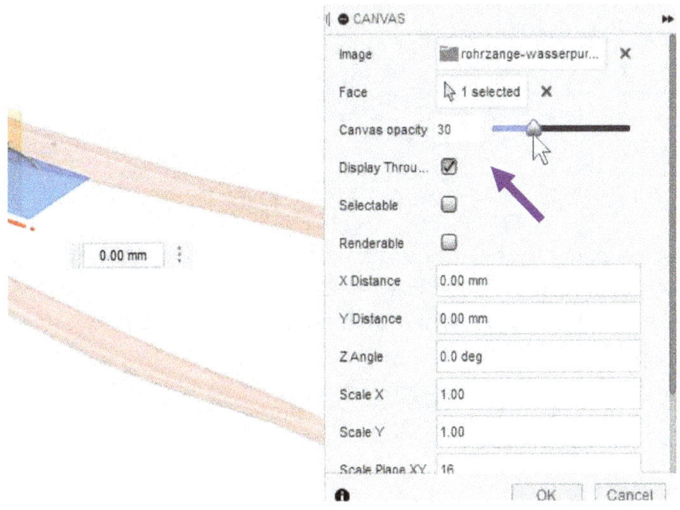

We thus have our template in the program, which we will trace step by step and use to create the tongs. We will create the first sketch on the x-y plane. If we now briefly consider how the pincer is created, we see that it consists of two interlocking components, which we call legs.

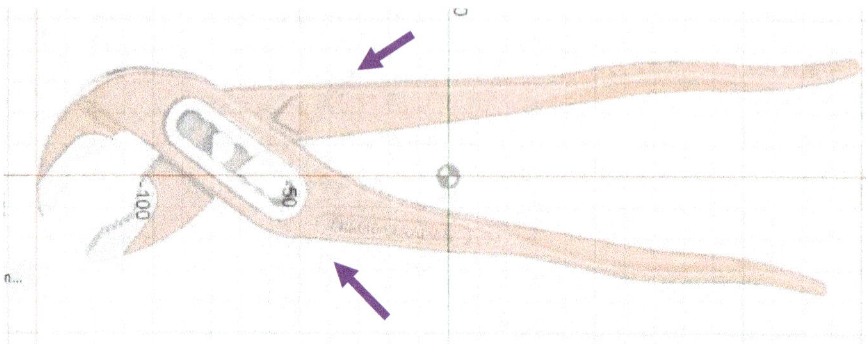

In this sketch, we will first trace one of the two legs of the pliers using lines and arcs on the outline edges. We start with the middle section of the first component, where the adjustment mechanism will be later. Now we simply draw individual lines as best we can and as accurately as possible using the outline edges as shown.

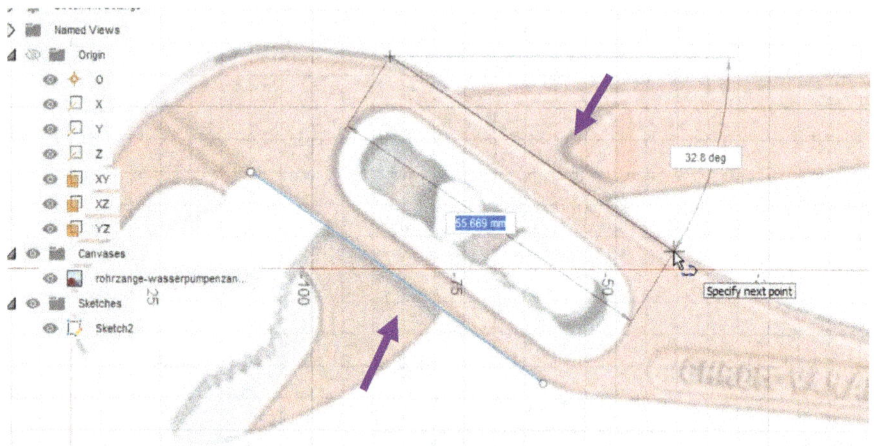

We can first reproduce the outline using simple lines. Later we can add fillets. For strong fillets like in this area, we can also use a 3-point arc. In the front area of the pliers, we try to recreate the zigzag pattern of the pliers jaws as best we can with lines.

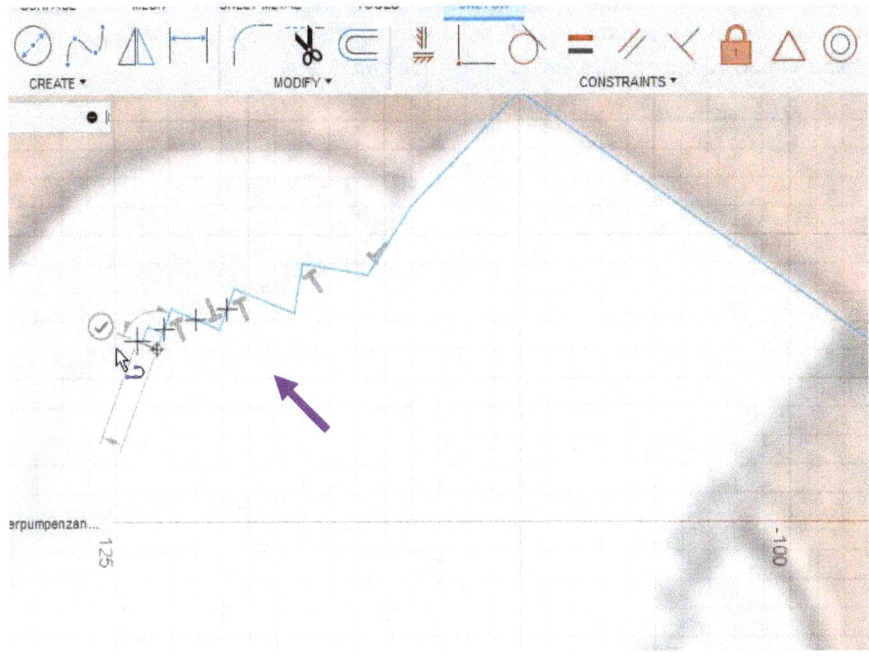

Depending on the scaling and image quality, however, you won't be able to see much here and will have to draw freehand as best you can. We then close the upper area of the first component again with a 3-point arc.

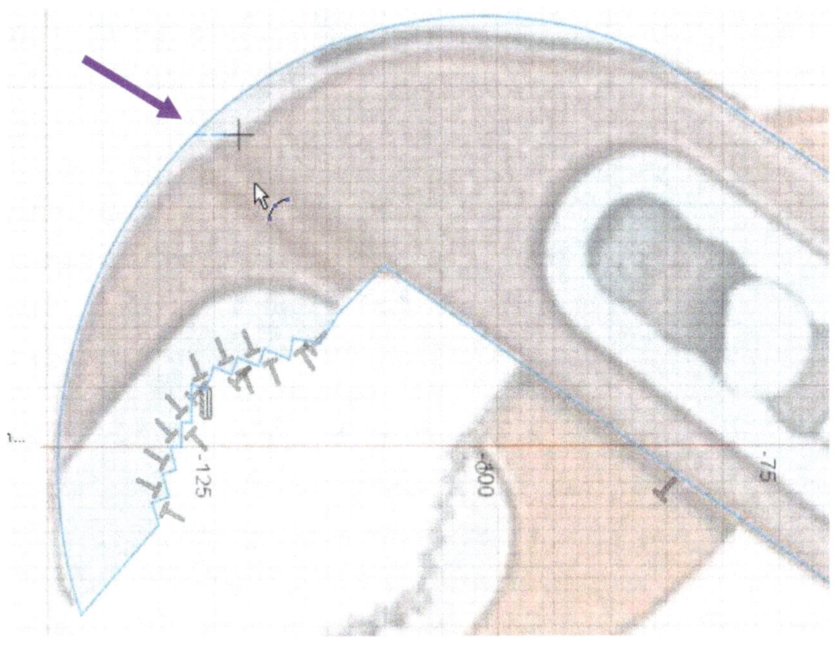

In the next step, we add the already announced fillets to the still very angular profile shape. Simply round off here at your discretion and desire.

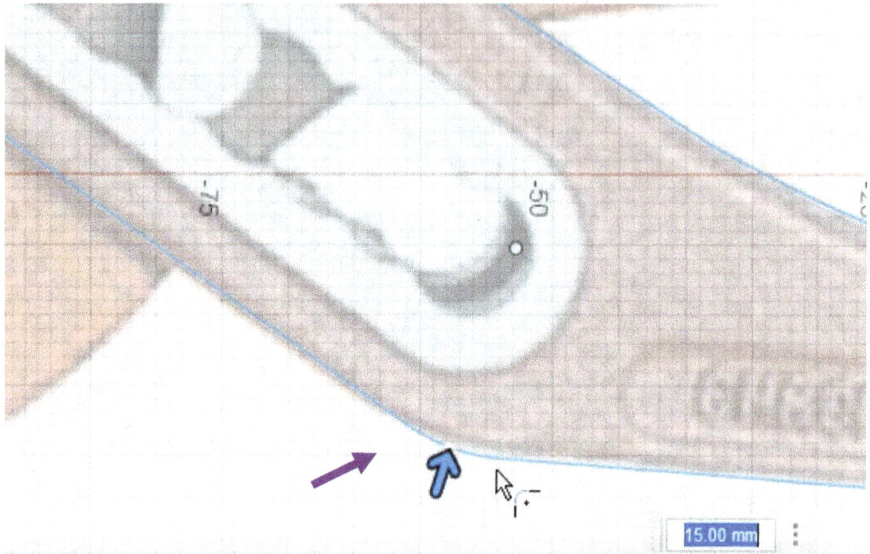

Thereafter, we create the middle area, which belongs to the adjustment mechanism of the pliers. We can create this relatively easily from several adjacent circles. Place the two outer circles as best you can. A design line should connect these two circles at their centers.

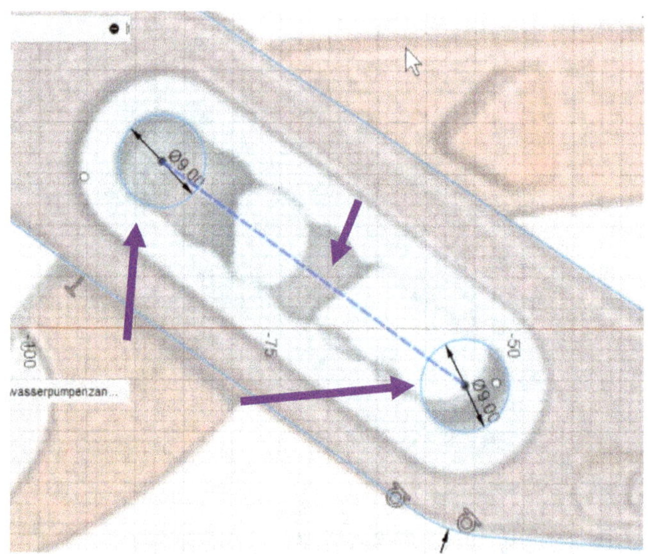

We create all other circles with the "Rectangular Pattern" command. To do this, we select the first circle and then switch to "Directions" in the settings so that we can determine the direction. We do this by selecting the design line. The command is then executed along this direction. We increase the number and spacing so that the circles are approximately congruent with the image.

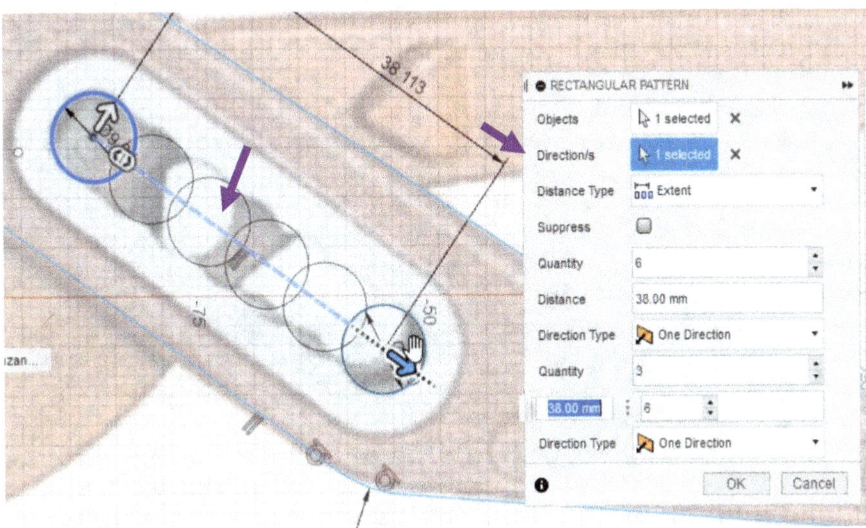

Now we have to remove the superfluous arc segments with the "Trim" function.

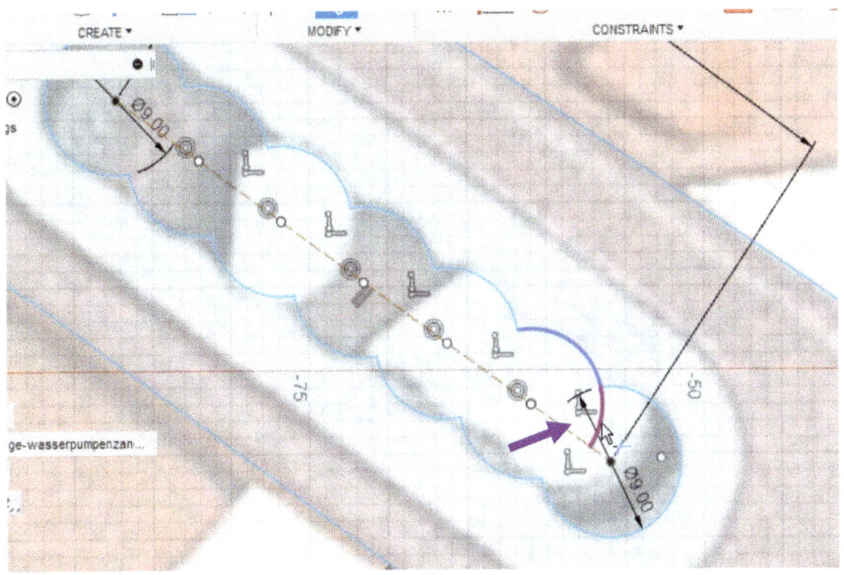

Now we already have a first rough sketch of the cross-section geometry of the first component. We could now refine this with a complete dimensioning. You are welcome to do this as a diligence task. However, since it would unnecessarily lengthen the scope of the course, we will not create any dimensions here and will content ourselves with the roughly sketched geometry, which is also perfectly adequate for our purposes. We will completely define the sketched geometry in a different way. We will use the "Fix" relationship from the "Constraints" section after we have selected all sketch elements.

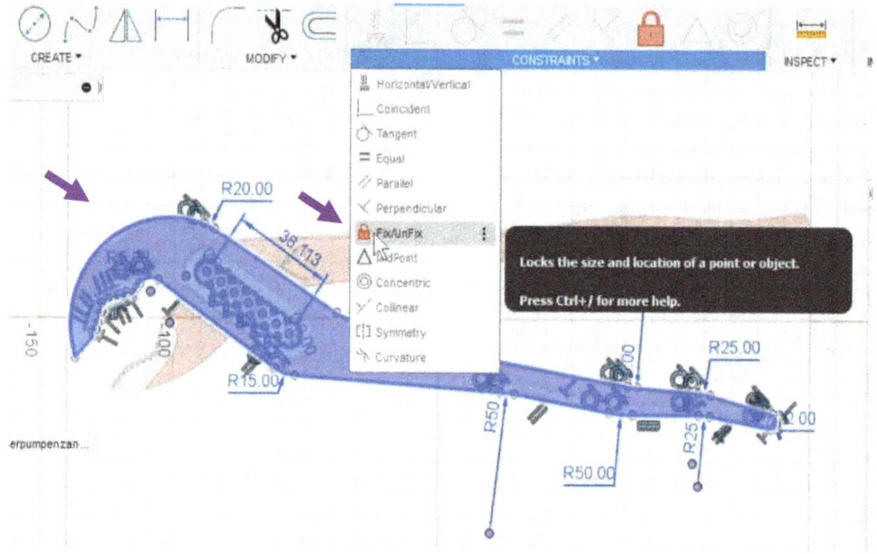

Now nothing can be moved. We can now extrude the sketched profile 10 mm. It is best to use symmetrical extrusion again to have the x-y plane in the component.

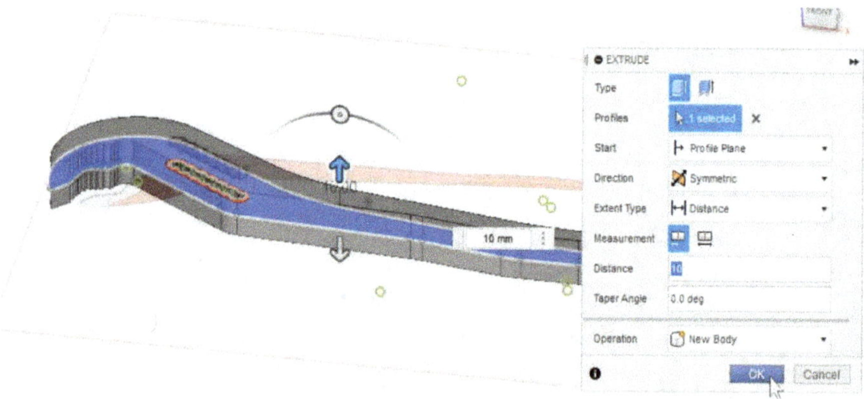

With this, the first leg of the pliers is almost ready. However, we still need two adjustments. First, we need a cutout in the area of the pliers head, which is easily created with a 3-point rectangle on the face and the "Extrude" function.

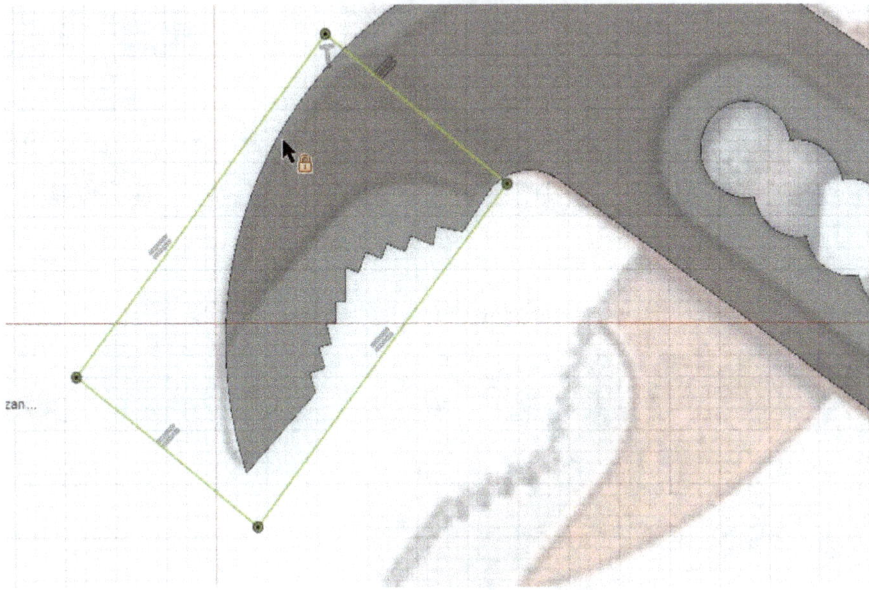

In this case, we choose, for example, a dimension of - 3.5 mm.

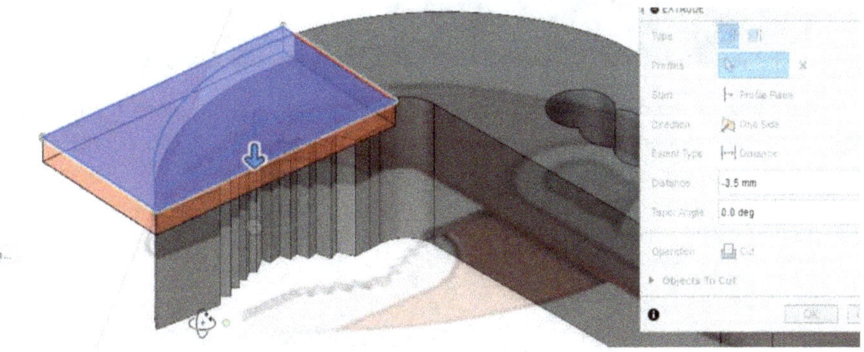

Since we also need this section on the other side, we mirror it on the x-y plane.

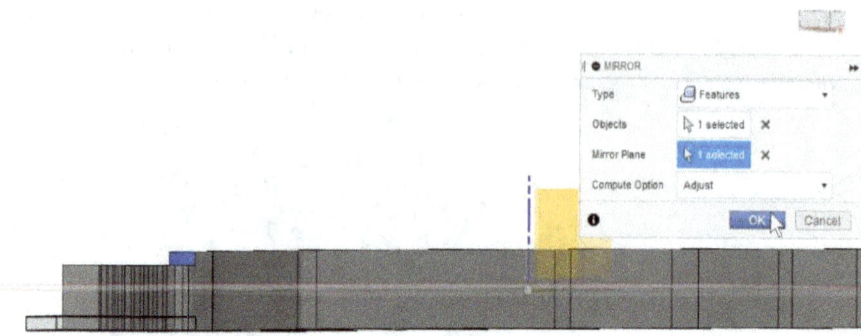

In the transition area, we can create fillets of 2 mm each.

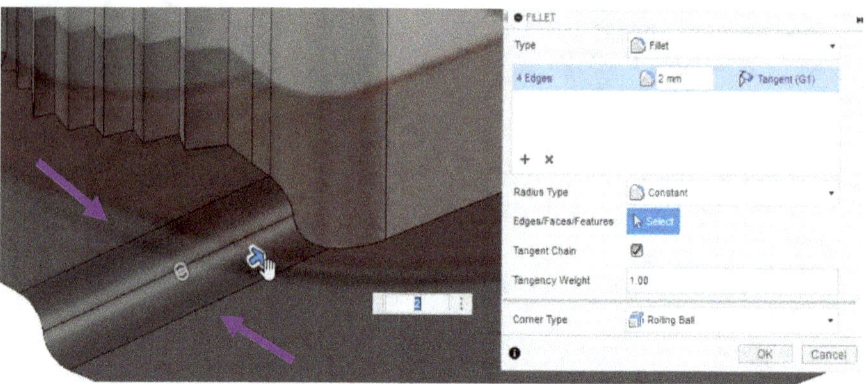

The last thing we need is a cutout in the middle segment of the first component, where the second component will sit. We create this by creating a rectangular profile on the back surface, which we then extrude using the "Cut" option.

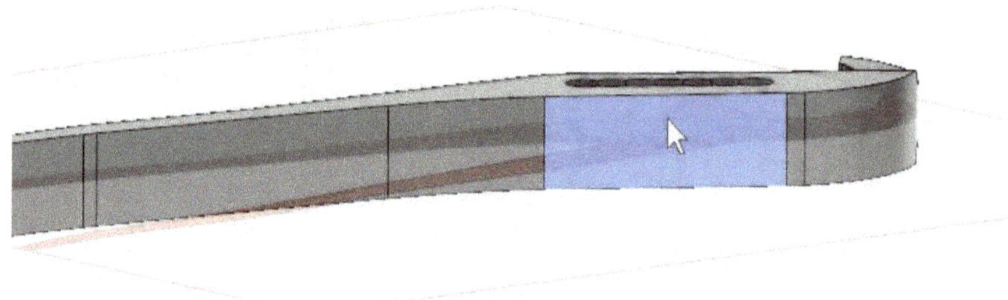

We first create the dimensions of the profile by feel and will later adjust them to the second leg of the pliers.

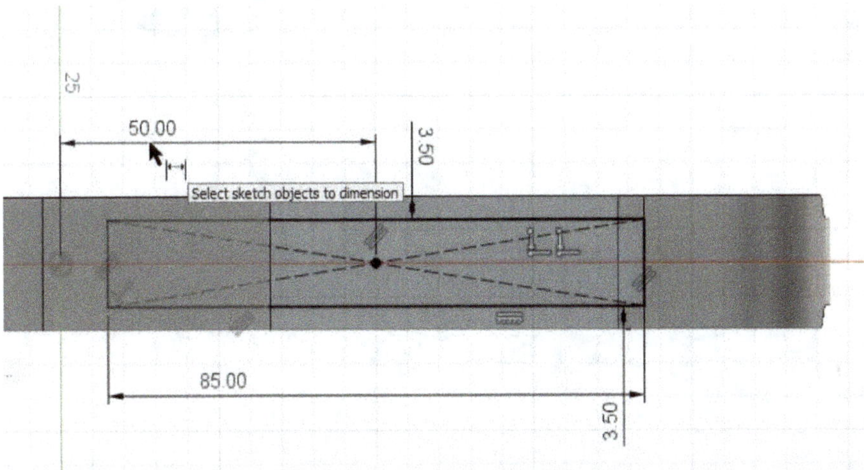

To select the profile, we can also temporarily hide the body.

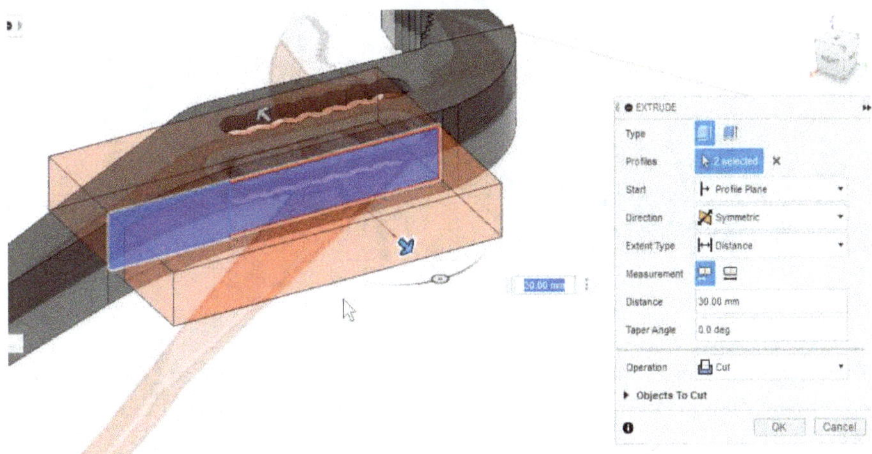

Now the first leg of the pincer is ready, and we can create the second leg in the identical way. But first we need to create a new component. On the x-y plane of the new component, we then draw the second profile. If the image is too transparent in this step, we can change this value again with a right click on the image and "Edit" at "Opacity".

We then use the outline again to draw the cross-section geometry of the component using lines and arcs. After adding fillets as well, we can finish the sketch and extrude the profile symmetrically in 3D mode.

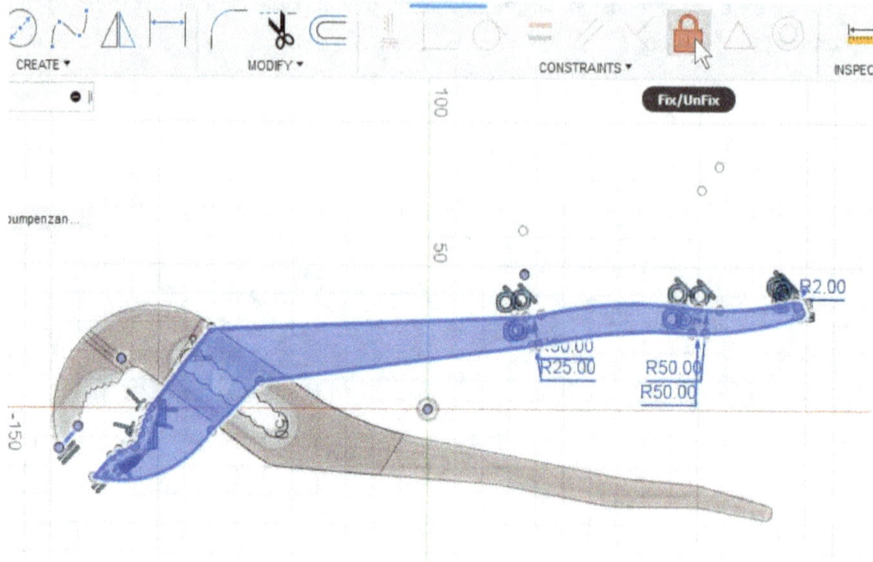

In our case, we need a dimension of 6.25 mm.

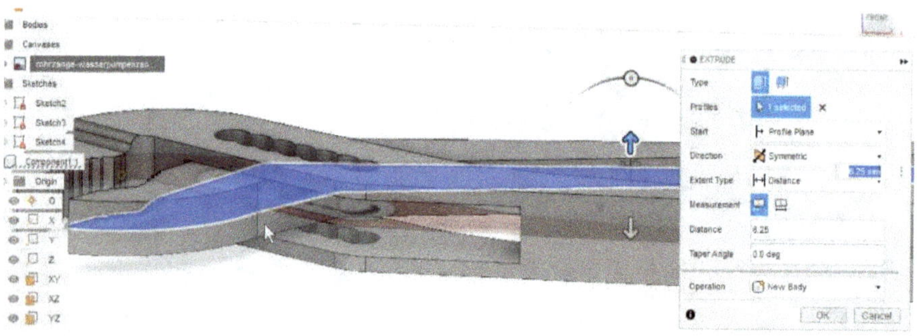

Then the second leg of the pliers is also almost ready. We still need two elements: the adjustment mechanism in the middle and a triangular element for the stop.

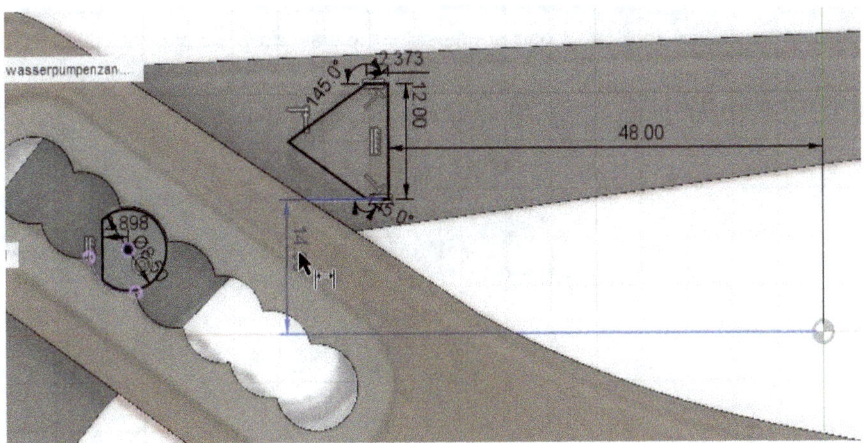

We create this with a sketch and an extrusion. Not only that, but we want the extrusion to go all the way to the top surface of the other component, so in the settings for "Extent Type" we select: "To Object" and then simply select this surface.

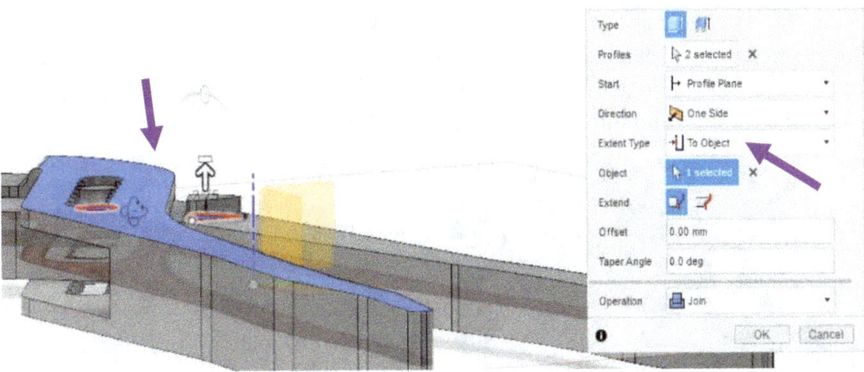

We need these two elements on the other side as well, so we mirror them on the x-y plane. If mirroring – as it is the case for me and maybe also for you right now – does not work once, select the option "Identical" instead of "Adjust" at "Compute Option" in the settings. Then it should work.

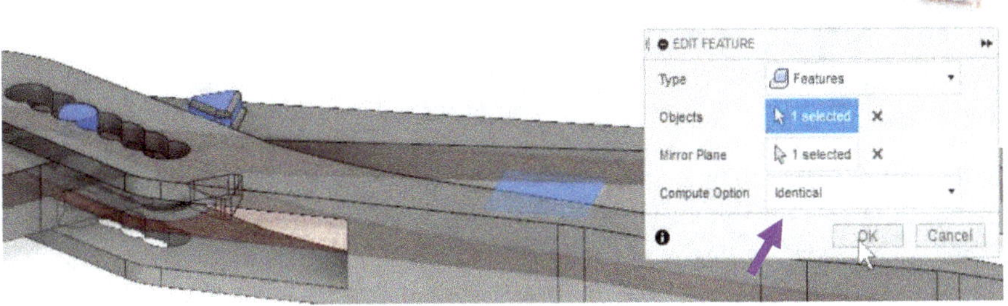

Meanwhile, it does look like a pair of pliers. By the way, if the body of the pliers is in the wrong component folder, you can easily drag it into the correct component in the part browser, as you can see here:

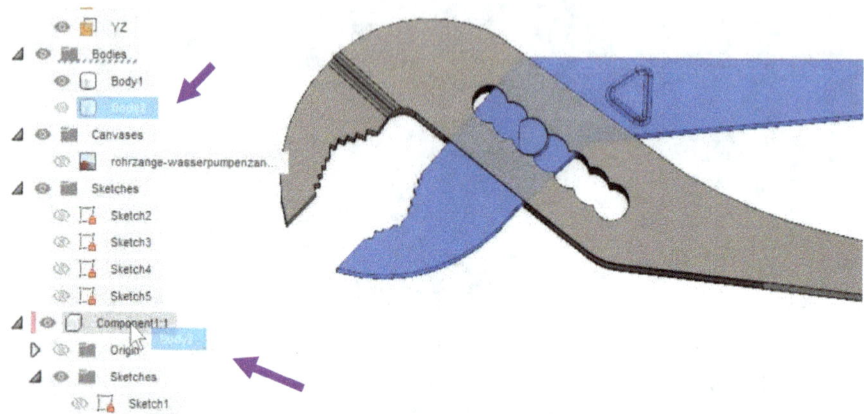

Excellent, now we want to link the two legs of the pliers with a joint. To do this, we select the round pin of the adjustment mechanism and one of the holes provided for it in the other component. Set the joint origins as shown and select the joint type "pin slot" for a rotation and a linear movement option.

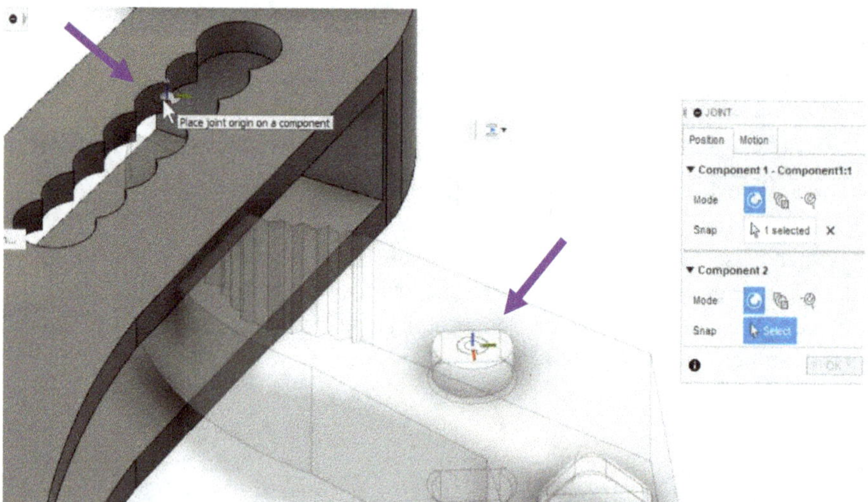

In the settings, we can now adjust the axes for the movements. The rotation axis "z" fits, but the axis for the linear movement is not correct in this case. We therefore change the "Slide" setting in the joint settings to "Custom" and simply click on the lateral edge of the pincer, which runs parallel to our direction of movement.

With a right click on the joint and "Edit Joint Limits" we can then define the joint limits. In this case, we can set two limits each for the rotation and the linear movement. You can switch between the joint types using the drop-down menu in the settings. For "Slide" we set for the minimum e.g., -12.5 mm and for the maximum e.g., 25.5 mm.

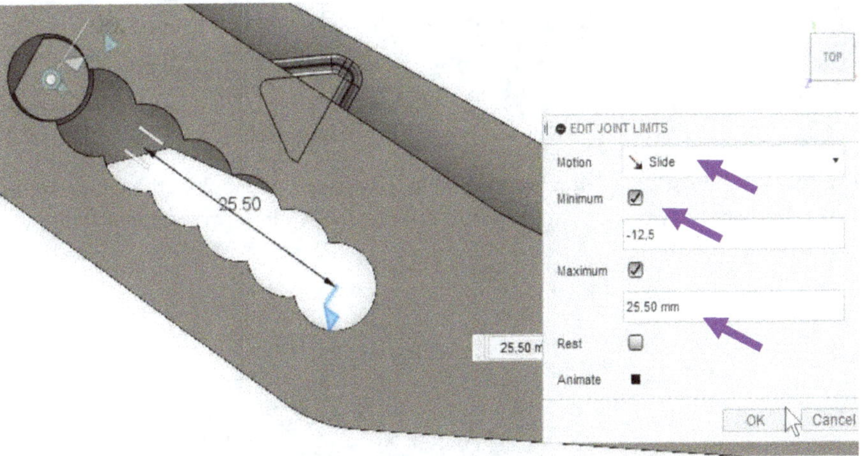

For the time being, we limit the rotation to -2 degrees in the minimum and +65 degrees in the maximum. We may have to fine-tune this later.

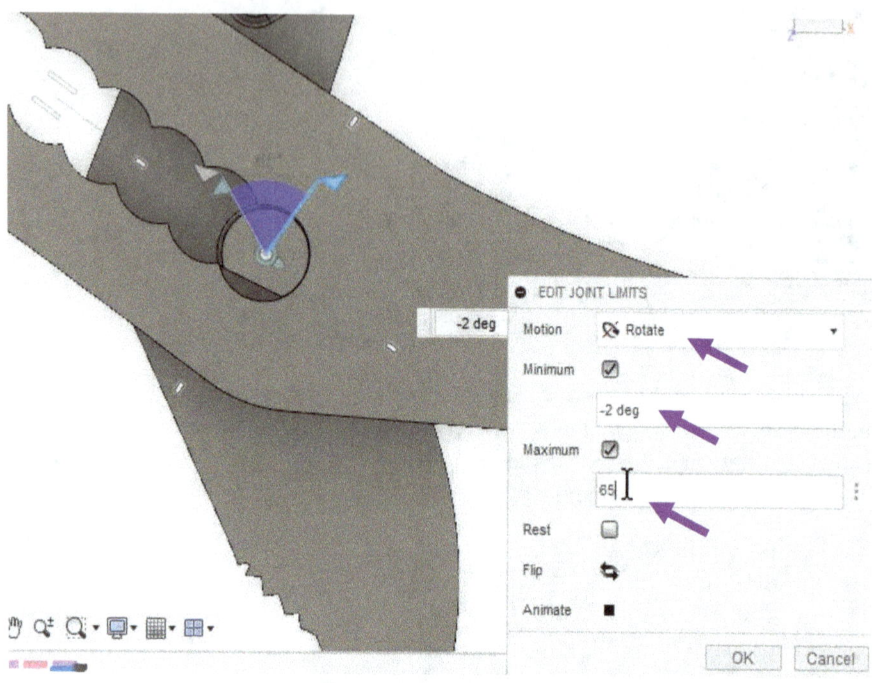

Now we are almost done. However, we have to take another look at the cutout of the first component because as we can see, it does not yet fit in terms of dimensions.

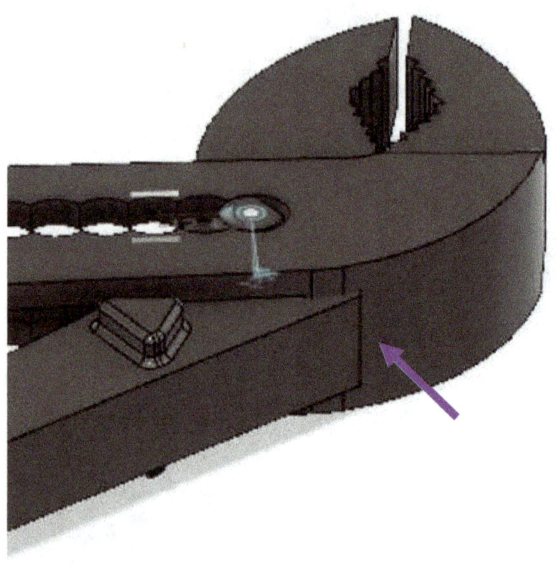

We resize and move the rectangular profile until the second component has enough space to move freely.

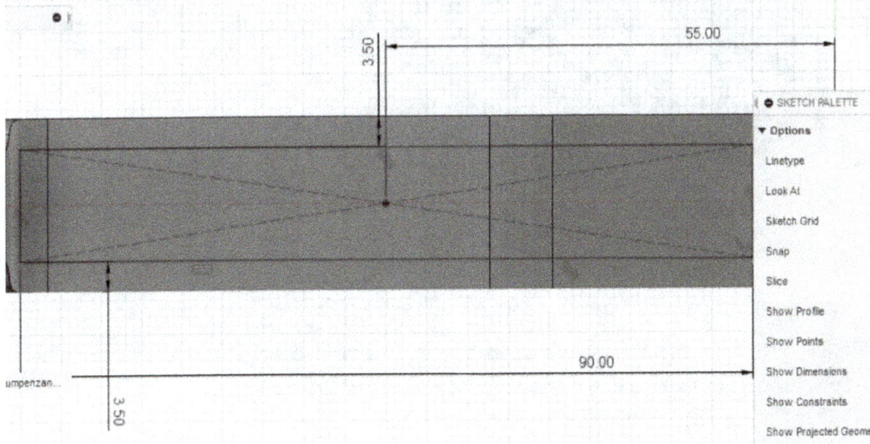

Then we also adjust the limits of the rotation of the joint once again. In this case, -4 degrees for the "minimum" and +25 degrees for the "maximum" fit better.

Then we round some edges according to taste and desire.

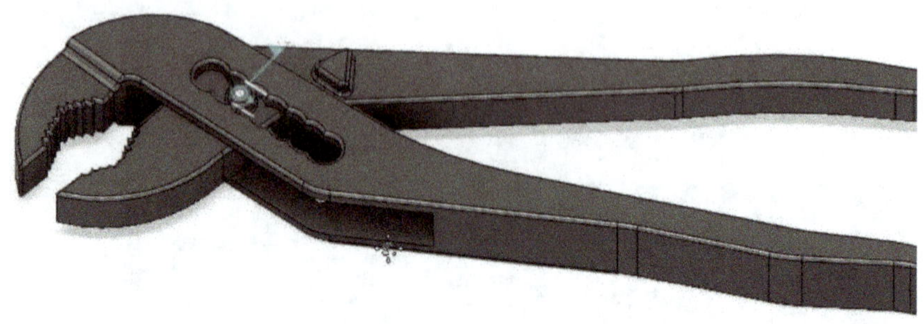

Finally, we hide the image we used for tracing and change the appearance with Appearance. For example, we could choose a red metallic paint.

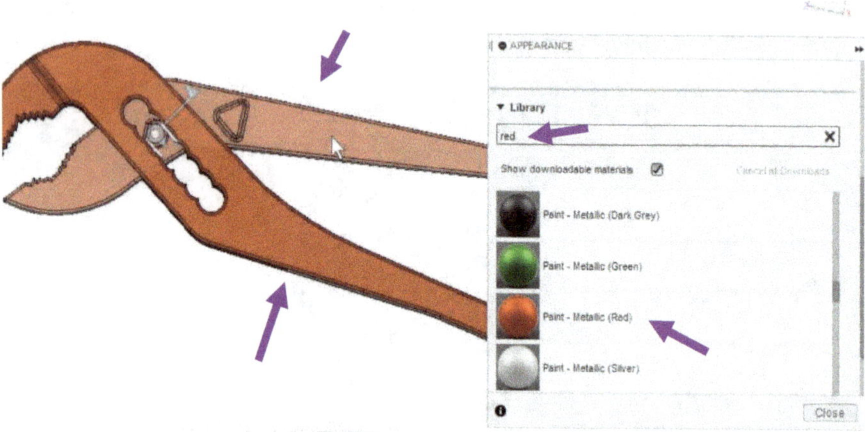

Then the pliers are ready! With a right click on the joint and the selection of "Animate Model" we can also see the adjustment mechanism of the pliers in action.

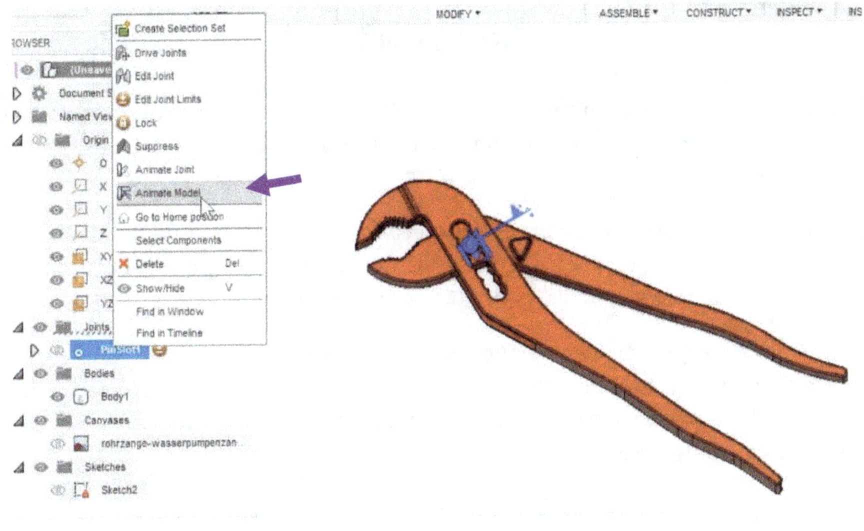

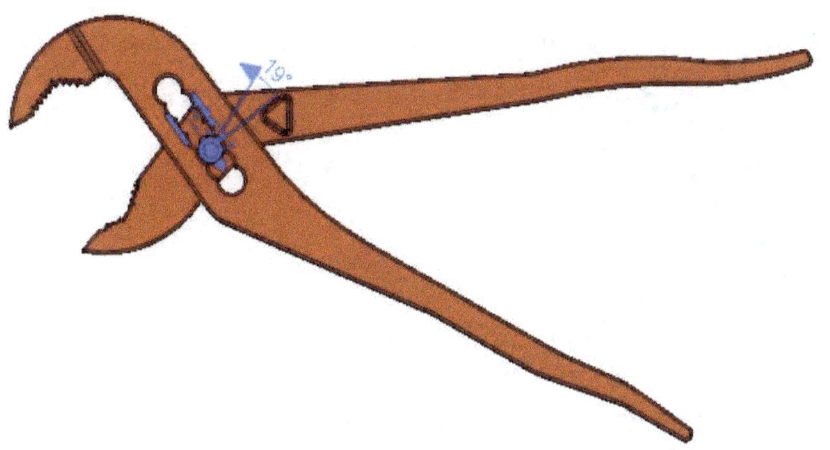

The animation can then be ended again with the ESC key. Perfect! We are done with the design projects!

Closing words

Excellent! You did it, with this chapter we finish the first part of the advanced course for CAD in Fusion 360! By now, you should already have good skills in CAD design with Fusion 360.

Together, we have designed many great objects in this course, learned new functions and deepened the basics. So, we've accomplished quite a bit! Be justifiably proud of yourself if you've made it to this lesson! Congratulations!

As you may have guessed by now, there will also be a second part to this CAD design course, which is similarly structured and covers moderately difficult to complex design objects. You are welcome to take a look at the sequel as well! Then you can almost see yourself as a professional!

And if you also want to experience your design objects for real in 3D, be sure to take a look at 3D printing as well. It's tremendously fun and beneficial to be able to materialize your designs.

The best way to do this is to use my course:

"3D Printing | 101" and get started today!

If you enjoyed the advanced CAD design course in Fusion 360, I would personally be pleased if you leave me a rating and a short feedback, as well as recommend the course! This will also help other interested persons in their decision. Thank you very much and see you soon.

Books on topics you might also like

All books are available online on the usual sales platforms. It's best to just search for the title, or feel free to visit my author page. Some books may not be published yet and will be released or found soon. Take a look at the books of your choice and your copy as e-book or paperback!

3D Printing:

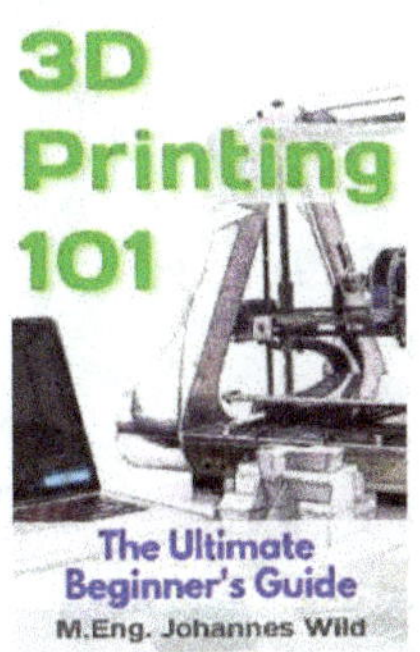

CAD, FEM, CAM (3D Object Creation, Design, Simulation):

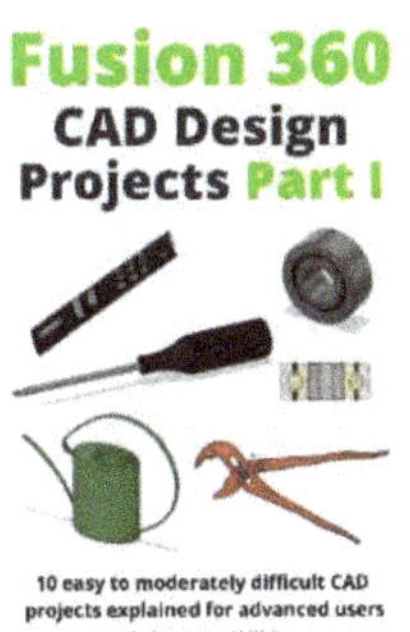

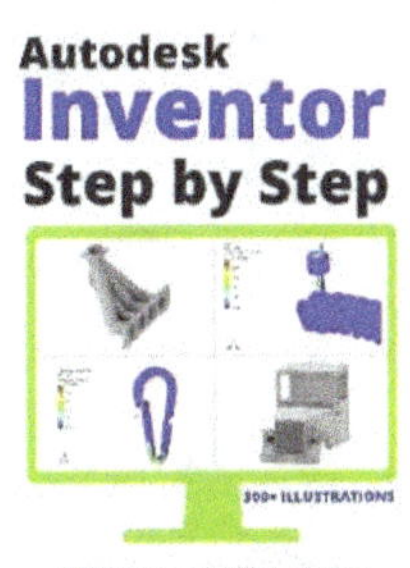

Electrical Engineering:

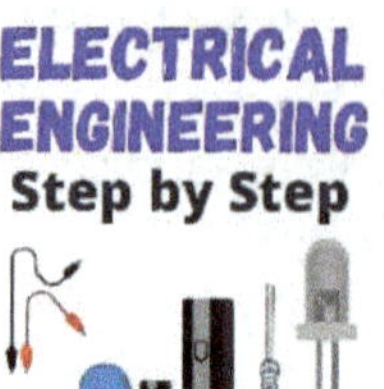

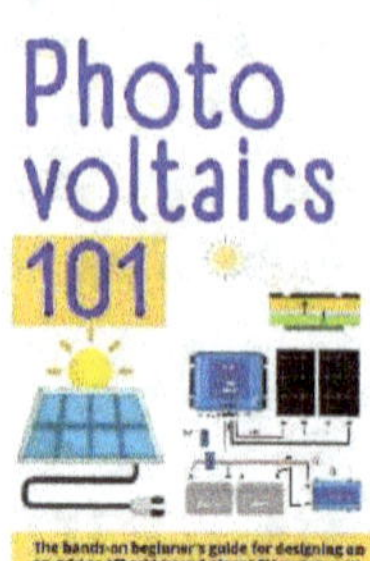

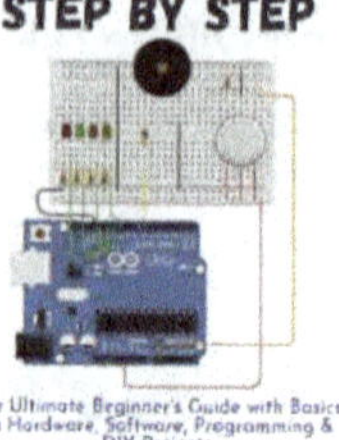

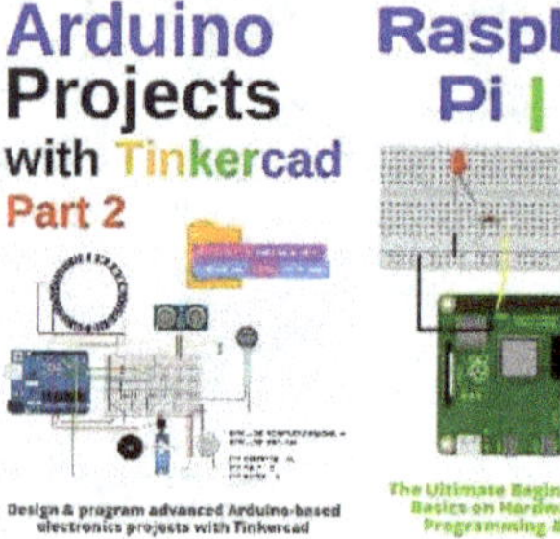

Programming and other Software:

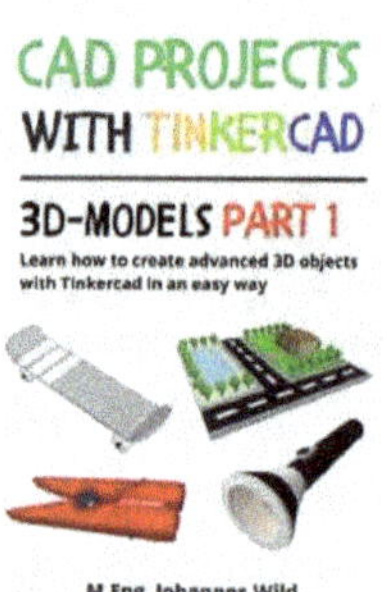

There are also identical video courses for some of these books:

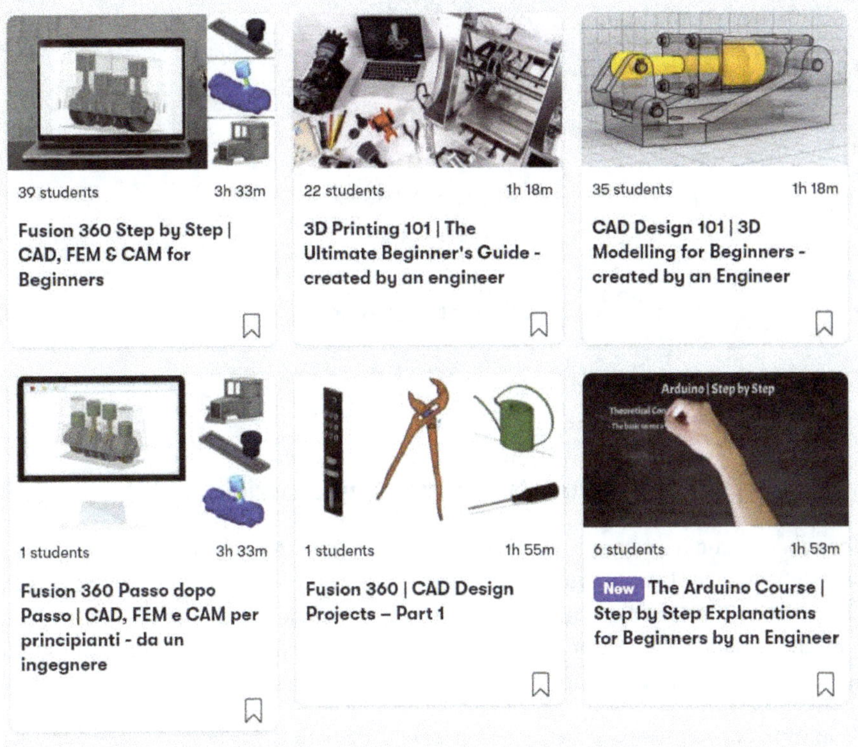

They are hosted on the learning website: skillshare.com

Be sure to use my following friends & family referral link to get a month of membership for free !

(I will get a little bonus if you choose to stay, so we will be both happy. Thanks in advance!)

https://www.skillshare.com/r/profile/Johannes-Wild/854541251

It is best to copy the link in your browser to access the free month !

Sign up today and deepen your knowledge!

Imprint of the author / publisher

© 2023

Johannes Wild
c/o RA Matutis
Berliner Straße 57
14467 Potsdam
Germany

Email: 3dtech@gmx.de

This work is protected by copyright

Thank you so much for choosing this book!